Henry,

Thanks –

Seis Lagos
Mens Club

1

Order extra copies now!

Cowboys' fans, friends, memorabilia collectors, and good cooks
that you know will love a copy of this limited-edition

"COOKIN' WITH THE COWBOYS"
HAPPY HILL FARM ACADEMY/HOME
HC 51, BOX 56
GRANBURY, TEXAS 76048

*****Please Make Your Check or Money Order Payable to:*****
HAPPY HILL FARM

(or)

Telephone: (817) 897-4822 to place your order on

 or

Single Copy $16.95 + $2.95 Shipping/Handling ($19.90 Total)

SPECIAL LIMITED OFFER "CB-3"
3 BOOKS TO ONE ADDRESS, $49 POSTPAID
(save over $10)

This is my
"Cookin' with the Cowboys" order

WRITE CHECK OR MONEY ORDER TO:
"HAPPY HILL FARM"

___ Send me one copy ($16.95 + $2.95 s/h) $19.90 total enclosed

___ Send me two copies ($33.90 + $5.90 s/h) $39.80 total enclosed

___ **Rush "Special Offer CB-3" -- 3 copies, $49 POSTPAID**

Name _____

Address _____

City, State, Zip _____

___ Optional. Please use this extra donation of $ _____ to help Happy Hill Farm **Academy/Home**
care for troubled, hurting children. (Happy Hill Farm does not receive any government funds,
but depends entirely on voluntary gifts from the public to do its work.)

"Why do you do this?"

IT'S NOT JUST A FUN PROJECT. IT'S A LOT OF HARD WORK . . . BUT THE ANNUAL COOKBOOK LITERALLY MEANS ANOTHER CHANCE IN LIFE FOR TROUBLED, NEEDY BOYS AND GIRLS.

NO ONE IN THE DALLAS COWBOYS' ORGANIZATION MAKES A PENNY ON THE COOKBOOK. ALL OF THE FUNDS RAISED GO DIRECTLY TO THE CHILDREN AT HAPPY HILL FARM ACADEMY/HOME.

Thousands of America's children are in trouble. Teenage violence is rampant. Drug and alcohol abuse are epidemic. Aids is spreading among teenagers. Children are being abused and neglected. Unmarried young girls -- mere children themselves -- are having babies. Many are born addicted. These kids need help.

That's why there is a Happy Hill Farm Academy/Home. Nestled in the hill country southwest of the Dallas-Fort Worth Metroplex, for 20 years the Farm has been a haven for hundreds of these hurting children.

**"COOKIN' WITH THE COWBOYS" raises funds
for the kids at Happy Hill Farm Academy/Home.**

HAPPY HILL FARM ACADEMY/HOME DOES NOT RECEIVE ANY STATE OR FEDERAL FUNDS, NO UNITED WAY MONIES, NOR FINANCIAL SUPPORT FROM ANY CHURCH DENOMINATION. ALL GIFTS ARE FROM THE PRIVATE SECTOR -- PEOPLE JUST LIKE YOU.

Write or call today:

**HAPPY HILL FARM ACADEMY/HOME
HC 51, Box 56
Granbury, Texas 76048
Phone: (817) 897-4822**

Happy Hill Farm Academy/Home

SPONSORS
for the

1995
"COOKIN' WITH THE COWBOYS"

Family Photo Album and Favorite Recipes of the Dallas Cowboys

(compiled by the Dallas Cowboys' Wives)

Our Grateful Appreciation to our SPONSORS from the Students at HAPPY HILL FARM ACADEMY/HOME

THE AD PLACE

BOB AND MARY BREUNIG

DAVID MCDAVID AUTO GROUP

FRICASSE FINE COOKWARE

FRIENDLY CHEVROLET - DALLAS

INTERSTATE BATTERIES

INCREDIBLE UNIVERSE

NATIONAL DOOR INDUSTRIES, INC.

NETWORK GRAPHICS

SMILEY'S STUDIO

TOM THUMB/SIMON DAVID/RANDALLS

WALLS INDUSTRIES

We're on a roll to extend our commitment to quality community partnerships through our support of
Happy Hill Farm

We're happy to help with your recipe for success.

Happy Hill Farm Recipe

- Take one child
- Add patience and understanding
- Mix in kindness
- Blend in a strong family unit
- Add a healthy helping of Christian values
- Sprinkle with discipline
- Top off with a solid education
- Season with plenty of love

Note: This recipe has served hundreds of children, but with additional support could serve many other boys and girls who still need help.

Walls

LEADING THE WAY OUTDOORS

Auto Group

Dallas   Austin   Houston

11

12

All of us at

Interstate Batteries

are pleased to continue our support of

Happy Hill Farm

and the Dallas Cowboys Wives' Cookbook.

*We're proud to be associated with
an organization that provides a warm
and caring, Christian atmosphere for
children who need it most.*

Official sponsor of the NFL

Bob & Mary Breunig

Supporting
the children at

Happy Hill Farm
Academy/Home

since 1978

WIN!

A Chantal Kitchen Absolutely FREE!
Courtesy of FRICASSEE Fine Cookware

Long-lasting German porcelain enamel. Carbon steel core for faster heat. For all cooking surfaces, including induction. Ideal for stir-fry. Stunning hand-crafted Italian glazed ceramics. Color-coordinated with Chantal Cookware and Canisters. Unique windows, seal-tight lids, and classic, contemporary design. Made of powder-coated steel, Chantal Canisters are lightweight and easy to handle.

> *INCLUDING:*
> *8 Piece Set*
> *5 Piece Bowl Set*
> *Large Mixing Bowl*
> *3 Piece Canister Set*
> *Large Canister*
> *Spoon Holder*
> *Utensil Holder*
> *Stir Fry*

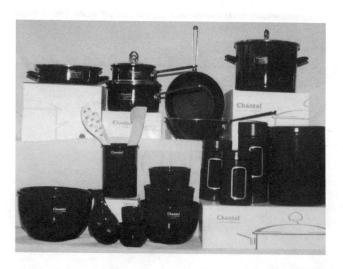

Name
Address
City
State, Zip
Telephone (H)
Telephone (W) _____ Age ____

Drop by in person or mail

780 S. MacArthur Blvd.
Suite 160
Coppell, TX 75019
(214) 304-0535

Drawing will be held Saturday, February 3, 1996. You do not need to be present to win.

COOKIN' with the
COWBOYS

Family Photo Album
and
Favorite Recipes
of the
Dallas Cowboys

(Compiled by the Dallas Cowboys' Wives)

Happy Hill Farm Academy/Home
HC 51, Box 56
GRANBURY, TEXAS 76048
(817) 897-4822

Copyright 1995

HAPPY HILL FARM ACADEMY/HOME
HC 51, BOX 56
GRANBURY, TEXAS 76048

COOKIN' WITH THE COWBOYS
(FAMILY PHOTO ALBUM AND FAVORITE RECIPES
OF THE DALLAS COWBOYS)

First Printing: October, 1995

Printed in the United States of America

Printed by
HORTICULTURE PRINTERS, INC.
Dallas, Texas

All of the proceeds from this cookbook go directly to the Scholarship Fund at Happy Hill Farm Academy/Home, supporting deserving boys and girls (ages 5-18), who live, work, and study on the 500-acre working-farm campus -- located just outside the Dallas-Fort Worth Metroplex. The Farm is licensed by the Texas Department of Human Services and accredited by the Southern Association of Colleges and Schools. Happy Hill Farm does not receive any State or Federal funding.

TABLE OF CONTENTS

ACKNOWLEDGEMENTS

Players, coaches, and Cowboys administration, and their wives, have teamed up again this year to produce the biggest and best, all-new **"COOKIN' WITH THE COWBOYS."** This year's volume contains all-new recipes, plus many photos of the players, coaches, administrators, wives, and families . . . more pictures than ever before.

It's best not to list names, for invariably someone will be left out . . . but to each Cowboys' wife who was a part of our "inner circle" of workers, our heartfelt gratitude. Without you, there would be no book.

To all of the wives, players, and coaches who had a part in the production of the book . . . **THANKS!**

Again, our "special thanks" to Yvette Novacek, who gave leadership to the effort. Yvette and Jay wrote letters, made phone calls and personal appearances, and much more. We are very grateful.

Our gratitude to Charlotte (Jones) Anderson, who directs the Special Events Office -- and to her able assistant, Doreen Bice, without whose cooperation the project could not have been accomplished.

Special thanks, also, to Kevin and Anne O'Neill.

Tammy and Chad Hennings -- our sincere thanks!

The cover photography, along with other photos used in marketing and promotion, were taken by "Smiley" Irvin -- Smiley's Studio -- located in Fort Worth, Texas.

Our gratitude to Gary and Linda Lawrence of Network Graphics (Fort Worth, Texas), for all scanning and film output.

Design concepts and art for the book cover were produced by The Ad Place in Dallas, Texas. Special thanks to Earl Calhoun, Tracy Watson, and artist, Steve Hahn.

ACKNOWLEDGEMENTS -- (continued)

Items for the cover photography were courtesy of Tom and Missy Whitenight, owners of Fricassee Fine Cookware in Coppell, Texas.

Our appreciation to Russ Russell, Jim Browder, and Bobby Collier -- of the "Dallas Cowboys Weekly" -- in allowing the use of "Weekly" photographs to fill in a few picture gaps.

John Chang, and his capable Cowboys' television staff, provided their time and expertise in the production of the cookbook television public service announcement.

The Cowboys' public relations staff -- Rich Dalrymple and Emily Cruz, along with Brett Daniels and Doug Hood -- were always gracious in providing information and pictures.

The Jones family, and the Dallas Cowboys organization, graciously cooperated in providing needed information and the use of the Cowboys' logo.

To all of our friends in the Front Office, we are grateful -- especially to Marylyn Love and Laura Fryar.

My sincere gratitude and appreciation to Gloria, my wife, and our son, Todd, who set the type (Gloria typed over 500,000 characters on the computer!). Together they layed out and edited the cookbook, doing all the things necessary for production.

Again, to "everyone who did anything" to make this year's volume, "COOKIN' WITH THE COWBOYS", become a reality, we are very grateful.

What you all have done is very, very important. Scholarship funds raised from "COOKIN' WITH THE COWBOYS" will mean another chance in life for troubled, needy children.

C. Edward Shipman
Executive Director
HAPPY HILL FARM ACADEMY/HOME

The Dallas
COWBOYS
AT HAPPY HILL FARM
ACADEMY/HOME
**"Where, since 1975, deserving boys and girls live,
work, and study, free from abuse and neglect."**

DEDICATED OCTOBER 7, 1995

THE SIXTH HOME TO OPEN NEAR AN NFL CITY AS PART OF A NATIONAL NETWORK FOR ABUSED CHILDREN

Through the compassion and concern of Jerry Jones, the Dallas Cowboys, Cowboys Alumni, and the unswerving commitment of Head Athletic Trainer Kevin O'Neill, the **DALLAS COWBOYS COURAGE HOUSE at HAPPY HILL FARM ACADEMY/HOME** is now a reality.

This concept of the Courage House National Support Network for Abused Children is the mission of the **ED BLOCK COURAGE AWARD FOUNDATION** in Baltimore. Their goal is to dedicate a Courage House in or near each of the NFL cities. To date there are six Courage Houses: Baltimore, Pittsburgh, Chicago, Miami, Detroit, and Dallas.

The partnership embodied within the Courage House logo represents the commitment of the NFL, NFL Charities, NFL Alumni, Players Association, PFATS, and the **ED BLOCK COURAGE AWARD FOUNDATION.** The commitment is to provide shelter, treatment, and prevention programs to victims of child abuse and domestic violence.

Kevin O'Neill, Ed Shipman,
Jay Novacek, and Lee Hitt

Happy Hill Farm children with
Bill Bates and Bob Breunig

:h year, the Ed Block Courage Awards honor those National
)tball League players who exemplify commitment to the
nciples of sportsmanship and courage. They are selected by
mmates for team effort as well as individual performance.

DALLAS COWBOYS RECIPIENTS OF
THE ED BLOCK COURAGE AWARD

1984 - JAMES JONES
1985 - HOWARD RICHARDS
1986 - ANTHONY DORSETT
1987 - BRIAN D. BALDINGER
1988 - RANDY WHITE
1989 - ED "TOO TALL" JONES

1990 - KELVIN MARTIN
1991 - KEN NORTON, JR.
1992 - DARYL JOHNSTON
1993 - BILL BATES
1994 - MARK STEPNOSKI

TOP: Ed Shipman, Lee Hitt, Mary Jones, and Mike Montgomery

MIDDLE: Lee Hitt, Mark Stepnoski, Ed Shipman, and Mike Montgomery

BOTTOM: Mark Stepnoski with Gloria and Ed Shipman, Founders/Directors of Happy Hill Farm Academy/Home

nks to efforts – like the **Dallas Cowboys Courage House** –
s and girls at **Happy Hill Farm Academy/Home** are being
wed to break the cycle of abuse and neglect and to prepare
mselves academically, emotionally, spiritually, and
itionally for successful young adulthood.

1995 DALLAS COWBOYS

OWNER/PRESIDENT and GENERAL MANAGER (WIF

Mrs. Jerry Jones (Gene)

EXECUTIVE VICE PRESIDENT / DIRECTOR OF PLAYER PERSONNEL (WIFE)

Mrs. Stephen Jones (Karen)

VICE PRESIDENT / DIRECTOR OF MARKETING and SPECIAL EVENTS

Mrs. D. Shy Anderson (Charlotte Jones)

HEAD COACH

Barry Switzer

VETERAN PLAYERS' WIVES

Mrs. Larry Allen (Janelle)
Mrs. Reggie Barnes (Eulanda)
Mrs. Bill Bates (Denise)
Mrs. Larry Brown (Cheryl)
Mrs. Scott Case (Connie)
Mrs. Dixon Edwards (Secola)
Mrs. Cory Fleming (Tracey)
Mrs. Jason Garrett (Brill)
Mrs. Charles Haley (Karen)
Mrs. Dale Hellestrae (Brooke)
Mrs. Chad Hennings (Tammy)
Mrs. Michael Irvin (Sandy)
Mrs. John Jett (Jacque)
Mrs. Robert Jones (Maneesha)

Mrs. Derek Kennard (Denise
Mrs. Brock Marion (Keri)
Mrs. Russell Maryland (Rose
Mrs. Godfrey Myles (Janice,
Mrs. Nate Newton (Dorothy)
Mrs. Jay Novacek (Yvette)
Mrs. Deion Sanders (Carolyi
Mrs. Jim Schwantz (Brenda
Mrs. Tony Tolbert (Tasha)
Mrs. Mark Tuinei (Pono)
Mrs. Kevin Williams (Tina Howe
Mrs. Wade Wilson (Kathy)
Mrs. Darren Woodson (Juli)

SINGLE VETERAN PLAYERS

Troy Aikman
Michael Batiste
Chris Boniol
Shante Carver
Anthony Fieldings
George Hegamin
Clayton Holmes
Daryl Johnston

David Lang
Leon Lett
Hurvin McCormack
Emmitt Smith
Kevin Smith
Ron Stone
Greg Tremble
Erik Williams

1995 DALLAS COWBOYS

SINGLE ROOKIES

Eric Bjornson
Alundis Brice
Billy Davis
Edward Hervey
Oscar Sturgis
Kendell Watkins
Charlie Williams
Sherman Williams

COACHING STAFF'S WIVES

Mrs. Hubbard Alexander (Gloria)
Mrs. Neill Armstrong (Jane)
Mrs. Joe Avezzano (Diann)
Mrs. John Blake (Freda)
Mrs. Joe Brodsky (Joyce)
Mrs. Dave Campo (Kay)
Mrs. Jim Eddy (Sharlene)
Mrs. Robert Ford (Janice)
Mrs. Steve Hoffman (Raffy)
Mrs. Hudson Houck (Elsie)
Mrs. Ernie Zampese (Joyce)
Mrs. Mike Zimmer (Vikki)

SINGLE COACHES

Craig Boller
Mike Woicik

OTHER COWBOYS STAFF'S WIVES

Mrs. Robert Blackwell (Diana)
Mrs. Bucky Buchanan (Amy)
Mrs. Rich Dalrymple (Ros)
Mrs. Larry Lacewell (Criss)
Mrs. Jim Maurer (Rosanne)
Mrs. Bruce Mays (Kathy)
Mrs. Mike McCord (Jan)
Mrs. Kevin O'Neill (Anne)

#55 -- Robert Jones   **#40** -- Bill Bates   **#84** -- Jay Nova

#8 -- Troy Aikman   **#88** -- Michael Irvin

ADMINISTRATION

Gene and Jerry Jones with grandson, *Shy* Anderson, Jr.

GENE & JERRY JONES

PERSONAL DATA

DALLAS COWBOYS FRONT OFFICE
Owner/President and General Manager

BORN: *Jerral (Jerry) Wayne* -- 10-13-42 in Los Angeles, California; *Gene* -- 2-14-42 in Little Rock, Arkansas

HIGH SCHOOL: *Jerry* -- North Little Rock High School

COLLEGE: *Jerry* -- University of Arkansas (Masters -- Business Administration); *Gene* -- University of Arkansas (Liberal Arts)

FAVORITE TYPE OF MUSIC: *Jerry* -- Country/western; *Gene* -- Broadway scores

FAVORITE FOOD: *Jerry* -- Popcorn; *Gene* -- Cookies

FAVORITE AUTHOR: *Jerry* -- Tom Clancy; *Gene* -- John Grisham

FAVORITE SPORTS HERO: *Jerry* -- Vince Lombardi; *Gene* -- Husband Jerry

HOBBIES AND INTERESTS: *Jerry* -- Tennis, water skiing, snow skiing, hunting, and playing with grandchildren; *Gene* -- Being with family, snow skiing, walking the beach, and charity involvement

CHILDREN AND AGES: Stephen - 31 yrs.; Charlotte Jones Anderson - 29 yrs.; and Jerry, Jr. - 26 yrs.

GRANDCHILDREN AND AGES: Jessica Jones - 3 yrs.; Jordan Jones - 2 yrs.; Haley Anderson - 2 yrs.; and Shy, Jr. - 6 months

TOP: Papa and his "little princess" -- at Jessica's third birthday party!

BOTTOM: Christmas, 1994 -- *(back row)* Haley Anderson (1-1/2 years) with Papa, Jerry Jones, and *(front row)* Gene Jones with granddaughters, Jordan (1 year) and Jessica (2 years).

GENE & JERRY JONES

ATHLETIC and ACHIEVEMENTS DATA

DALLAS COWBOYS FOOTBALL CLUB
Owner/President and General Manager

PURCHASE OF DALLAS COWBOYS: February 25, 1989

ATHLETIC HONORS OR AWARDS: *Jerry* -- Starred in football as a running back at North Little Rock High School; received scholarship to play at the University of Arkansas; starting guard and co-captain of 1964 national championship Razorback football team (11-0)

ACHIEVEMENTS (HONORS OR AWARDS): *Jerry* -- Boys Club Award; awarded Best Sports Franchise Owner in the Metroplex in 1991; Edelstein Pro Football Letter NFL Owner of the Year in 1991; in 1992 -- "Big D Award" by the Dallas All Sports Association - ESPY Award for NFL Team of the Year - Golden Plate Award from American Achievement Academy - Field Scovell Award - Business Leader of the Year - Waterford Crystal Trophy for Super Bowl Championship - appointed to NFL's prestigious Competition Committee in May, becoming the first owner to serve in that capacity since the late Paul Brown; in 1993 -- Entrepreneur of the Year, presented by Ernst and Young and "Inc." magazine - member of NFL's Broadcasting Committee - following 1993 season, Cowboys appeared in an NFL-record seventh Super Bowl; in 1994 -- was one of ten national winners of the Entrepreneur of the Year Award presented by Ernst and Young and "Inc." magazine - named one of America's Ten Most Interesting People in a nationally-televised Barbara Walters special on ABC; in 1995 -- "Financial World" magazine recognized Jones as the owner of the most valuable sports team in all of professional athletics - only owner (out of 17 who have entered NFL in past 16 years) to guide his franchise to a Super Bowl championship (or two!); Jones ranked 26th in "The Sporting News" list of the 100 Most Powerful People in Sports for 1995; *Gene* -- 1992 Arkansas Woman of Distinction; TACA Executive Board; Board member of Children's Medical Center of Dallas; Mental Health Center; Willis M. Tate Distinguished Lecture Series; Easter Seals; member of Symphony and Dallas Museum of Art

TOP: "Cheering on the 'Boys" (September, 1995) -- Karen and Stephen Jones with daughters, Jessica (3 years) and Jordan (2 years).

BOTTOM: Jessica and Jordan at breakfast time with Dad -- Summer, 1995.

STEPHEN & KAREN JONES

PERSONAL DATA

DALLAS COWBOYS FRONT OFFICE
Vice President/Director of Player Personnel

BORN: *Stephen* -- 6-21-64 in Danville, Arkansas; *Karen* -- 8-9-64 in Warren, Arkansas

HIGH SCHOOL: *Stephen* -- Catholic High School in Little Rock

COLLEGE: *Stephen* -- University of Arkansas (Chemical Engineering); *Karen* -- University of Arkansas (Business Administration)

WIFE'S OCCUPATION: Wife and mother

FAVORITE TYPE OF MUSIC: *Stephen* and *Karen* -- Country and pop

FAVORITE FOOD: *Stephen* -- Steak, pizza, and pasta; *Karen* -- Italian

FAVORITE AUTHOR: *Stephen* -- John Grisham; *Karen* -- John Grisham and Sidney Sheldon

FAVORITE SPORTS HERO: *Stephen* -- Roger Staubach; *Karen* -- Husband Stephen

CHILDREN AND AGES: Jessica - 3 yrs.; and Jordan - 2 yrs.

PETS: Golden Retriever -- "Maggie"

FITNESS AND DIET TIP: Jogging, low-fat diet, and MET-Rx

TOP: Jessica on her third birthday at her party in August, 1995.

BOTTOM: Ready for a swim! Jessica (3 yrs.) and Jordan (2 yrs.) in summer, 1995.

STEPHEN JONES

ATHLETIC and ACHIEVEMENTS DATA

DALLAS COWBOYS FOOTBALL CLUB
Vice President/Director of Player Personnel

YEARS IN PROFESSIONAL FOOTBALL: 7th year as an NFL executive

ENJOY MOST ABOUT BEING WITH THE DALLAS COWBOYS: Working in sports on a daily basis

HONORS OR AWARDS: *Stephen* -- All-State quarterback and three-year starter at Catholic High School; four-year letterman as a linebacker and special teams stand-out at Arkansas; named vice president of the Cowboys in February, 1989; as Director of Player Personnel, oversees the handling of all player contracts and the daily management of the salary cap; recognized as owner Jerry Jones' right-hand man, Stephen also directly supervises the administration of Texas Stadium and a wide assortment of other club-related duties; in summer of 1992, was the key figure in the negotiation and signing of 13 veteran contracts, enabling the Cowboys to start the season with a complete roster in their run to the Super Bowl title; in 1993, was instrumental in contract dealings that eventually made Troy Aikman, Emmitt Smith, and Daryl Johnston the highest paid players at their respective positions in NFL history; has enjoyed a life-long association with the game of football, and over the past six years has surfaced as one of the NFL's rising young stars on the executive level

Charlotte Anderson with children, Shy Anderson, Jr., and Haley.

CHARLOTTE (JONES) & SHY ANDERSON

PERSONAL DATA

DALLAS COWBOYS FRONT OFFICE
Vice President/Director of Marketing and Special Events

BORN: *Charlotte* -- 7-26-66 in Springfield, Missouri; *Shy* -- 4-3-63 in Little Rock, Arkansas

COLLEGE: *Charlotte* -- Stanford University (B.A. -- Organizational Management and Human Biology); *Shy* -- University of Arkansas (B.A. -- Business)

ENJOY MOST ABOUT BEING WITH THE DALLAS COWBOYS: *Charlotte* -- The excitement of the entertainment business and the great personalities of the individuals we work with

HUSBAND'S OCCUPATION: Vice President/General Manager -- Alltel Mobile of Arkansas

FAVORITE TYPE OF MUSIC: *Charlotte* -- Contemporary; *Shy* -- Country/western

FAVORITE FOOD: *Charlotte* and *Shy* -- Pasta and Mexican

FAVORITE AUTHOR: *Charlotte* -- Sidney Sheldon and Jeffrey Archer; *Shy* -- Michael Crichton and Tom Clancy

FAVORITE SPORTS HERO: *Charlotte* -- Father, Jerry Jones

HOBBIES AND INTERESTS: *Charlotte* -- Skiing, hunting, exercising, and being a mom; *Shy* -- Golf, hunting, and exercising

CHILDREN AND AGES: Haley Alexis - 2-1/2 yrs.; and Shy, Jr. - 6 months

TOP: Haley and Shy, Jr.

BOTTOM: Jerry Jones, Jr., with Jordan Jones and Shy Anderson, Jr.

Haley and her daddy, Shy Anderson.

TOP: Barry Switzer, Head Coach of the Dallas Cowboys, with daughter, Kathy.

BOTTOM: Greg, Kathy, and Doug Switzer.

BARRY SWITZER

PERSONAL and ATHLETIC DATA

DALLAS COWBOYS FOOTBALL CLUB
Head Coach

BORN: 10-5-37 in Crossett, Arkansas

COLLEGE: University of Arkansas (B.A. -- Business Administration)

BECAME HEAD COACH OF DALLAS COWBOYS: Barry Switzer became the third head coach in the history of the Dallas Cowboys on March 30, 1994

HONORS OR AWARDS: Graduated from high school in 1958 with an appointment to the United States Naval Academy and offers of football scholarships at the University of Arkansas and Louisiana State University; attended Arkansas, playing center and linebacker three years for the Razorbacks; elected captain as senior in 1959, year Arkansas reigned as Southwest Conference champion and Gator Bowl winner; spent two years in army, returning to Arkansas as B-Team coach and scout; 1964-1965 -- coached offensive ends; 1966 -- moved to Oklahoma as offensive line coach; in April, 1967, named offensive coordinator; took responsibilities of assistant head coach in 1970; as head coach of University of Oklahoma from 1973-1988, was guiding force behind one of the most dominant college football programs of all time; amassed a 157-29-4 career record, underscoring the long-term quality of winning that Switzer brought to coaching -- his .837 winning percentage is the fourth highest mark in college history; during 16-year tenure at Oklahoma, won three National Championships, 12 Big Eight titles, and was successful in 8 of 13 Bowl contests; coached one Heisman Trophy winner, one Defensive Player of the Year, and two Butkus Award winners; as Sooners' head coach, personally guided careers of more than 120 young men who were drafted into NFL; personal achievements include awards from Walter Camp Football Foundation, Big Eight Conference, NCAA District V, Washington Pigskin Club, "The Sporting News", "Football News", Associated Press, and United Press International; Switzer became just the third man to lead his team to a NFC Championship game as a rookie NFL head coach

CHILDREN AND AGES: Greg - 27 yrs.; Kathy - 26 yrs.; and Doug - 23 yrs.

TOP: Some of the Dallas Cowboys' wives at the American Bowl in Toronto, Canada – 1995; *(back row)* Keri Marion, Janice Myles, Maneesha Jones, Yvette Novacek, Brill Aldridge-Garrett; *(front row)* Pono Tuinei and Brooke Hellestrae.

BOTTOM: Dallas Cowboys coaches' wives having fun snorkeling – taken at the Pro Bowl in 1994; *(left to right)* Jan McCord, Rosanne Maurer, Anne O'Neill, Raffy Hoffman, and Amy Buchanan.

VETERANS

TOP: Troy playing uncle to niece and nephews on Memorial Day (Brady Foreman - 4 years; Drew Powell - 2 years; and Brooke Foreman - 6 years).

BOTTOM: Grand Opening of Planet Hollywood in Dallas (Summer, 1994). (From left) Troy, Bruce Willis, Bill Bates, and Daryl Johnston.

TROY KENNETH AIKMAN

PERSONAL DATA

BORN: 11-21-66 in West Covina, California

HIGH SCHOOL: Henryetta (Oklahoma) High School

COLLEGE: U.C.L.A. (Sociology)

FAVORITE TYPE OF MUSIC: Country

FAVORITE FOOD: Italian

FAVORITE AUTHOR: John Grisham

FAVORITE SPORTS HERO: Larry Bird

HOBBIES AND INTERESTS: Hanging with friends, water sports, and seadoos

SPECIAL INTEREST: Established the Troy Aikman Foundation in 1991 -- benefits children's charities in the Dallas-Fort Worth area. Proceeds from his annual golf tournament and from a children's book he wrote, entitled "Things Change", released in March, 1995, also aid his foundation. In 1995, the Foundation made a donation to Children's Hospital of Dallas for funding of "Aikman's End Zone," a 2,500 square-foot interactive playroom and education center for children staying at the hospital. Troy has served on numerous charity projects throughout the Dallas-Fort Worth Metroplex and in Oklahoma -- also supports Happy Hill Farm

SPECIAL APPEARANCES: Troy has made a number of guest appearances on network television shows, including "The Tonight Show" with Jay Leno; "The Late Show" with David Letterman; "Live with Regis and Kathie Lee"; and was a presenter at both the Country Music Awards in 1993 and the ESPN "ESPY" Awards in 1994

PETS: Fish (salt water aquarium)

FITNESS AND DIET TIP: Jogging and eating right

Troy Aikman has guided Dallas from the NFL cellar in 1989 to three consecutive NFC Championship Games and back-to-back titles in Super Bowl XXVII and XXVIII.

TROY KENNETH AIKMAN

ATHLETIC DATA

* Number 8 *
Quarterback - 6'4" - 228 lbs.

FIRST PLAYED ORGANIZED FOOTBALL: Eight
years old, played quarterback for Suburban "Hornets"

YEARS IN PROFESSIONAL FOOTBALL: 7th year

ENJOY MOST ABOUT BEING WITH THE DALLAS COWBOYS:
The friendships and camaraderie

HONORS AND AWARDS: All-State honors (Henryetta
(Oklahoma) High School; an All-America, finished UCLA
collegiate career as the third rated passer in NCAA history (led
Bruins to win both the Aloha Bowl and the Cotton Bowl);
Heisman Trophy Finalist, received MVP for Aloha Bowl and
Cotton Bowl, awarded Davey O'Brien Award, named College
Quarterback of the Year in 1988, and voted UPI and consensus
All-America in senior year; selected #1 Overall Draft Pick for
1989; named NFL All-Rookie in his first year; named to All-
Madden Team five years in a row; named the Offensive MVP for
Cowboys three years in a row; recipient of Jim Thorpe
Performance Award in 1992; NFL Professional Quarterback of
the Year in 1993; led Cowboys to two consecutive Super Bowl
championships; named the MVP of Super Bowl XXVII; ESPN's
Insider Quarterback of the Year 1993; has been one of five
finalists for NFL Man of the Year, honoring players for their
contributions to the community and philanthropic work off the
field; selected to the Pro Bowl for the fourth consecutive season;
named to the All-Time Oklahoma High School Football Team
and to Pat Summerall's and John Madden's All-Time Cowboys
Team in 1994; received Field Scovell Award, Byron White
Humanitarian Award, and has been a finalist in the Cowboys
Man of the Year for last four years; the NFL career postseason
record holder for completion percentage (68.9) and average gain
per attempt (8.56), has the second highest postseason
quarterback rating in NFL history at 103.8; has the four highest
single-game playoff completion percentages in club history and
the club record for postseason career 300-yard passing days
(4)

Janelle and Larry Allen on their wedding day.

JANELLE & LARRY ALLEN

PERSONAL DATA

BORN: *Larry* -- 11-27-71 in Los Angeles, California; *Janelle* -- 5-7-71 in Santa Rosa, California

HIGH SCHOOL: *Larry* -- Vintage High School in Napa, California

COLLEGE: *Larry* -- Sonoma State (Sociology); *Janelle* -- Santa Rosa (Criminal Justice)

FAVORITE ACADEMIC SUBJECT: *Larry* -- Sociology; *Janelle* -- Law

FAVORITE TYPE OF MUSIC: *Larry* and *Janelle* -- Oldies

FAVORITE FOOD: *Larry* -- Mexican; *Janelle* -- Italian

FAVORITE SPORTS HERO: *Larry* -- Jackie Slater; *Janelle* -- Husband Larry

HOBBIES AND INTERESTS: *Larry* -- Fixing up old cars; *Janelle* -- Traveling

CHILDREN AND AGES: Jayla Lee - 9 months

LONG-RANGE CAREER GOAL: Own our own family business, and be a college football coach

TOP: Larry and Jayla (6 months) -- daddy and his little girl out for a day together.

BOTTOM: Jayla Lee Allen -- 9 months old.

LARRY ALLEN

ATHLETIC DATA

* Number 73 *
Tackle - 6'3" - 325 lbs.

FIRST PLAYED ORGANIZED FOOTBALL: In junior year in high school as offensive tackle/defensive end for the Centennial "Apaches"

YEARS IN PROFESSIONAL FOOTBALL: 2nd year

HONORS OR AWARDS: Lettered in football as a freshman at Centennial High School in Compton, California, where he attended for one year; consensus All-America selection; participated in East-West Shrine Game and Senior Bowl; earned All-America honors following his last college season; Division 2 Lineman of the Year; first player ever drafted from Sonoma State when the Dallas Cowboys selected him in the second round; in 1994, forced into the spotlight at left tackle when Mark Tuinei was injured -- performed like a proven veteran, although only four games removed from playing college football, and received a game ball for his play; moved into the starting lineup when Williams was injured and lost for the season -- at right tackle spot; received a game ball for blocking in the Monday night victory at New Orleans, a game in which the Saints were held without a sack; received another game ball against Green Bay, when the Dallas offense picked up 450 total yards and Troy Aikman completed 23-of-30 passes for 337 yards; has the distinction of being the highest draft choice among starting Dallas' offensive linemen, and the highest Dallas has taken an offensive lineman since 1981; with 10 starts in 1994, tied Dallas record for regular season starts by a rookie offensive lineman and earned consensus All-Rookie honors

TOP: Eulanda and Reggie at Eulanda's 26th birthday party at Dave and Buster's in Dallas on September 2, 1995.

BOTTOM: Reggie and Eulanda Barnes on a skiing vacation in Beaver Creek, Colorado.

EULANDA & REGGIE BARNES

PERSONAL DATA

BORN: *Reggie* -- 10-23-69 in Arlington, Texas; *Eulanda* -- 9-2-69 in Tishomingo, Oklahoma

HIGH SCHOOL: *Reggie* -- South Grand Prairie (Texas) High School, a suburb of Dallas

COLLEGE: *Reggie* -- University of Oklahoma (Organizational Communication); *Eulanda* -- University of Oklahoma (Public Administration)

WIFE'S OCCUPATION: State Farm Insurance Fire & Casualty Adjuster

FAVORITE TYPE OF MUSIC: *Reggie* -- Variety; *Eulanda* -- Jazz and gospel

FAVORITE FOOD: *Reggie* -- Alaskan King Crab legs; *Eulanda* -- Vegetarian dishes

FAVORITE AUTHOR: *Eulanda* -- John Grisham

HOBBIES AND INTERESTS: *Reggie* -- Ride horses and fishing; *Eulanda* -- Reading and working out

CHILDREN AND AGES: Expecting first child around November 9, 1995

HOW MET SPOUSE: After study hall at the University of Oklahoma (sophomore year)

FITNESS AND DIET TIP: Eat low fat foods, drink lots of water, and maintain a weekly workout schedule

LONG-RANGE CAREER GOAL: Entrepreneur

Reggie Barnes -- a promising young player on special teams in 1995.

REGGIE BARNES

ATHLETIC DATA

* Number 56 *
Linebacker - 6'1" - 240 lbs.

FIRST PLAYED ORGANIZED FOOTBALL: In the third grade at Lyndon B. Johnson Elementary in Grand Prairie, Texas

YEARS IN PROFESSIONAL FOOTBALL: 2nd year

GREATEST MOMENT IN SPORTS: Being selected first-team All-Big Eight in junior year in college

HONORS OR AWARDS: Starred at South Grand Prairie High School; made 33 tackles as a freshman at Oklahoma; moved from outside linebacker to defensive end as a sophomore, making 43 tackles; as a junior, was first-team All-Big Eight with 73 tackles and nine sacks; second-team All-Big Eight selection as a senior, after recording 46 tackles and 7 sacks in 9 starts; as a rookie free agent, saw action in all 16 games, mostly on special teams -- one of only three rookies to see action in every game for the Pittsburgh Steelers, finishing second on the team with 13 special teams tackles; signed with the Dallas Cowboys on February 13, 1995

TOP: Denise and Bill Bates at Cookbook Kick-Off Party in 1994.

BOTTOM: *(left to right)* Hunter, Graham, baby Dillon, Brianna, and Tanner -- welcome Dillon home to the nursery (July, 1995).

DENISE & BILL BATES

PERSONAL DATA

BORN: *William Frederick (Bill)* -- 6-6-61 in Knoxville, Tennessee; *Denise* -- 1-25-60 in Nashville, Tennessee

HIGH SCHOOL: *Bill* -- Farragut High School in Knoxville

COLLEGE: *Bill* -- University of Tennessee (Economics); *Denise* -- University of Tennessee (B.A. - Interior Design)

WIFE'S OCCUPATION: Professional mom -- cook, nurse, bottle washer, taxi driver, maid, coach, therapist, and teacher

FAVORITE TYPE OF MUSIC: *Bill* -- Country and old rock; Denise -- Classical piano, country, and old rock

FAVORITE FOOD: *Bill* -- Chicken Stroganoff; *Denise* -- Pasta

FAVORITE AUTHOR: *Bill* -- Tom Clancy and John Grisham; *Denise* -- Sidney Sheldon

FAVORITE SPORTS HERO: *Bill* -- Bart Starr and Joe DiMaggio; *Denise* -- Husband Bill

HOBBIES AND INTERESTS: *Bill* -- Golf, fishing, and any sport there is to play; *Denise* -- Piano, arts and crafts (especially painting), kids' clothing, and president of the "Plano Area Mothers of Multiples"

CHILDREN AND AGES: Triplets -- Graham, Brianna, and Hunter - 6 yrs.; Tanner - 4 yrs.; and Dillon - 3 months

LONG-RANGE CAREER GOAL: Dude ranch in McKinney -- "Bill Bates' Cowboy Ranch" for corporate events, picnics, and private parties; new restaurant -- "Bill Bates' Cowboy Grill" in North Dallas (opened in September, 1995 -- * Recipes listed are from the restaurant)

TOP: *(back)* Bill, holding Dillon, and Denise; *(front)* Brianna, Hunter, Tanner, and Graham -- in front of new restaurant (9-1-95).

BOTTOM: Opening night at the "Bill Bates' Cowboy Grill" (September 1, 1995).

WILLIAM FREDERICK (BILL) BATES

ATHLETIC DATA

* Number 40 *
Safety - 6'1" - 210 lbs.

FIRST PLAYED ORGANIZED FOOTBALL: When eight years old as an offensive guard with the "Head Hunters"

YEARS IN PROFESSIONAL FOOTBALL: 13th year

ENJOY MOST ABOUT BEING WITH THE DALLAS COWBOYS: Having the opportunity to continue playing a competitive sport that I love!

HONORS OR AWARDS: Second-team All-Southeastern Conference honors in junior and senior seasons in college; captain of college team; the NFL Alumni Special Teams Player of the Year in 1983 and 1984; in 1985, Pro Bowl, and NFL Man of the Year finalist; All-Madden Team in 1987 through 1993; Bob Lilly Award in 1990, 1991, 1993, and 1994; the special teams captain since 1990; led team in special teams tackles in 1993 with 25; has more career regular-season tackles (654) and more interceptions in a Dallas uniform (14) than any other member of the Cowboys' roster; Father of the Year in 1993 of "Dallas' Best"; closed 1994 as the team's second leading tackler on special teams with 26 stops; named the NFC Special Teams Player of the Week and received a game ball after recording four kicking game tackles against Philadelphia in 1994; is first among the current players in career regular season games played as a Cowboys' player, with 171

Michael Batiste in training camp, 1995.

MICHAEL SEAN BATISTE

PERSONAL DATA

BORN: 12-24-70 in Beaumont, Texas

HIGH SCHOOL: Westbrook High School in Beaumont

COLLEGE: Tulane University - New Orleans (B.S. -- Chemical Engineering)

FAVORITE ACADEMIC SUBJECT: Mathematics (Calculus and Differential Equations)

FAVORITE TYPE OF MUSIC: Rhythm and blues

FAVORITE FOOD: Pinto beans, rice, and fried chicken

FAVORITE AUTHOR: R. A. Salvatore

FAVORITE SPORTS HERO: Reggie White

HOBBIES AND INTERESTS: Video games, tennis, basketball, movies, and socializing

HONORS AND AWARDS RECEIVED: Distinguished Catholic Student (1995)

PETS: None at present (wants to purchase a parrot in the future)

PET PEEVE: Frivolous conversation

FITNESS AND DIET TIP: Stay away from fried and fatty foods

LONG-RANGE CAREER GOAL: To have own corporation in engineering-related business

TOP: Michael Sean Batiste -- 3 years old.

BOTTOM: Michael -- at age 24 in May, 1995.

MICHAEL SEAN BATISTE

ATHLETIC DATA

* Number 68 *
Guard/Center - 6'3" - 295 lbs.

FIRST PLAYED ORGANIZED FOOTBALL: Started playing football in the fifth grade

YEARS IN PROFESSIONAL FOOTBALL: 1st year

GREATEST MOMENT IN SPORTS: Making the cut for the Cowboys

HONORS AND AWARDS: All-District selection in football at Westbrook High School in Beaumont (Texas); also lettered in basketball and track; had his most productive season as a sophomore at Tulane University, when he started all year and recorded 57 tackles (38 solo), with 3 sacks and 6 tackles for losses; in junior year, contributed 42 tackles (25 solo), with 4 sacks and 5 tackles for losses in 9 games as a starter at defensive tackle; started 10 games in senior year at left end or tackle, recording 40 tackles (25 solo) with 1 sack and 3 tackles for losses; spent 1994 training camp with Dallas, but was released prior to the final roster cutdown; signed with Dallas Cowboys on April 10, 1995

TOP: *(from left)* Linda (mom), Mike (brother), Chris, and Don (dad) -- after the Saints game last December.

BOTTOM: Chris and Abby Lambert (cousin) -- her 4-H recipe, "Crawfish Pistolettes" - used by Chris on show in Dallas before the Saints game last year.

CHRIS BONIOL

PERSONAL DATA

BORN: 12-9-71 in Alexandria, Louisiana

HIGH SCHOOL: Alexandria Senior High School

COLLEGE: Louisiana Tech University (working on degree in Civil Engineering)

FAVORITE TYPE OF MUSIC: Country

FAVORITE FOOD: Cajun food

FAVORITE AUTHOR: Robert Fulgham

FAVORITE SPORTS HERO: Coach Jim Valvano (late North Carolina State basketball coach)

HOBBIES AND INTERESTS: Flying (earned private pilot's license) and golf

SPECIAL INTEREST: Served as an escort for the Children's Center Fund Fashion Show in 1995; also, supported the Exchange Club Center for the Prevention of Child Abuse in Dallas/Fort Worth, serving as a celebrity waiter

PETS: Maltese -- "Doc Holiday"

FITNESS AND DIET TIP: Eat all the good food you can while you can, and exercise in the morning to start your day

LONG-RANGE CAREER GOAL: Really not sure yet, but wants to finish engineering degree and get a good job

TOP: Mike (brother) and Don (dad) are with Marie Boniol (grandmother) -- taken in December, 1995, at Alexandria Senior High Football Banquet.

BOTTOM: Chris' aunt, Shirley Sayes *(seated)* and Marie Boniol (grandmother) at benefit for Louisiana State Police Troop E's Grant-a-Wish Program.

CHRIS BONIOL

ATHLETIC DATA

* Number 18 *
Placekicker - 5'11" - 159 lbs.

FIRST PLAYED ORGANIZED FOOTBALL: When a freshmen in high school as a back-up wide receiver

YEARS IN PROFESSIONAL FOOTBALL: 2nd year

ENJOY MOST ABOUT BEING WITH THE DALLAS COWBOYS: Everyone who works here is easy to be around -- also, Dallas is a nice city in which to live

HONORS AND AWARDS: Hit 10-of-18 career field goals and 113-of-121 extra points in high school career; as senior, hit 34-of-35 PAT's and a 47-yard field goal, while averaging 41.8 yards per punt; holds virtually every kicking record at Louisiana Tech, ending collegiate career third on school's all-time leading scorer list, second among kickers, with 255 points; led team in scoring 3 of 4 years at Tech and was 50-of-81 on field goals (.617), including 5 from over 50 yards; in second collegiate game, hit career-long 55-yard field goal, second longest in school history in 1990 Independence Bowl; named All-Louisiana and Louisiana Freshman of the Year by Louisiana Sportswriters Association after hitting 17-of-24 field goals and 38-of-39 extra points; in first NFL game (season opener), as a rookie, hit season-high 4 field goals and 2 extra points -- 14 points were the most ever by a rookie kicker in his Dallas debut -- and hit first 9-straight career field goal attempts, second-longest streak of consecutive field goals made by a kicker in club history; finished sixth in the NFC in field goal percentage at 75.8%, breaking club rookie record of 72% in the process; from 40-yard-or-less, was 16-of-19 (84.2%) and at Texas Stadium hit 10-of-12 (83.3%); his 22 successful field goals were 2 shy of rookie mark of 24; for 1994 season, amassed 114 points, which fell just shy of club rookie record of 119; total points were good for third in NFC and sixth in NFL in scoring among kickers; averaged 61.2 yards (inside 9-yard line) on 83 kickoffs, including 2 touchbacks; led all NFL rookies in scoring and field goals in 1994

Larry Brown worked his way into the starting lineup in only his fourth professional game.

CHERYL & LARRY BROWN

PERSONAL DATA

BORN: *Larry* -- 11-30-69 in Los Angeles, California; *Cheryl* -- 5-20-69

HIGH SCHOOL: *Larry* -- Los Angeles High School

COLLEGE: *Larry* -- Texas Christian University (Criminal Law); *Cheryl* -- Prairie View A & M University (Major - Sociology; Minor - Social Work)

FAVORITE TYPE OF MUSIC: *Larry* and *Cheryl* -- Jazz and gospel

FAVORITE FOOD: *Larry* and *Cheryl* -- Mexican food

FAVORITE AUTHOR: *Larry* and *Cheryl* -- Maya Angelou

FAVORITE SPORTS HERO: *Larry* -- Marcus Allen; *Cheryl* -- Husband Larry

HOBBIES AND INTERESTS: *Larry* -- Golf, basketball, working out, and singing; *Cheryl* -- Reading, swimming, dancing, and singing

CHILDREN AND AGES: Kristen - 2 yrs.

Larry in action against the Philadelphia Eagles.

LARRY BROWN

ATHLETIC DATA

* Number 24 *
Cornerback - 5'11" - 186 lbs.

FIRST PLAYED ORGANIZED FOOTBALL: As a ten-year-old, played for the "Hawthornes"

YEARS IN PROFESSIONAL FOOTBALL: 5th year

ENJOY MOST ABOUT BEING WITH THE DALLAS COWBOYS: Being on a winning team

HONORS OR AWARDS: All-City selection in both football and track at Los Angeles (California) High School; named to the All-Southwest Conference and to the Blue-Gray All-Star Game following his senior season, earning Most Valuable Player honors; Brown's play in 1991 earned him consensus All-Rookie honors; in 1992, led the team in passes defensed (11), and his 30-yard interception return against Philadelphia was the longest of the season for Dallas; in Super Bowl XXVII, Larry recorded his second career-playoff interception and led the team with three passes defensed; was a key player in Cowboys' defense that held opponents to 194 yards per game through the air and limited opposing quarterbacks to 6 yards per pass attempt; anchored the right corner in the Dallas defense that surrendered only 172 passing yards and 269.6 total yards per game, ranking first in the NFL in both categories; finished third on the team with four interceptions and tied for third with 12 passes defensed; since drafted by Dallas in 1991, has missed only two starts in the last three years, starting 70 of the past 72 games at right cornerback; ranks second on the team with 34 passes defensed and third in interceptions with seven

TOP: Shante Carver -- defensive end from Arizona State.

MIDDLE: Shante -- signing an autograph in 1994.

BOTTOM: Carver is an extremely quick, speed pass rusher who plays with great intensity -- taken at Minnesota Vikings game in 1994.

SHANTE CARVER

PERSONAL and ATHLETIC DATA

* Number 96 *
Defensive End - 6'5" - 242 lbs.

BORN: 2-12-71 in Stockton, California

HIGH SCHOOL: Lincoln High School in Stockton

COLLEGE: Arizona State University (Criminal Justice)

YEARS IN PROFESSIONAL FOOTBALL: 2nd year

HOBBIES AND INTERESTS: Hosted his first golf tournament on May 25, 1995, in Stockton, California, with proceeds from the tournament benefiting the Pop Warner Youth Football Program in Stockton

HONORS OR AWARDS: Earned first-team All-State honors as a senior at Lincoln High School; the most prolific pass rusher in Arizona State history -- had already shattered school record for quarterback sacks by end of junior season; first-team All-America selection by Football Writers Association; first-team All Pacific-10 Conference as a senior; Arizona State's defensive MVP in both junior and senior seasons -- shared the award as a sophomore; Carver recorded double-figure sack totals in each collegiate seasons -- 10 as freshman - 11 as sophomore - 10 as junior - and 10 as senior; closed out Sun Devil career with 41 quarterback sacks for losses totaling 248 yards; had 20-or-more quarterback pressures in all but freshman year, while accounting for 59 tackles behind the line of scrimmage for losses totaling 299 yards; played in 44 straight games for Arizona State and started 34 of those games; first-round draft choice (23rd overall) in the 1994 NFL Draft; finished rookie season with five total tackles after playing in 10 of team's 16 regular season games

TOP: Scott Case -- signed in 1995 as a free agent after eleven seasons with the Atlanta Falcons.

BOTTOM: Case provides Dallas with immediate veteran help in secondary and on nickel defense.

CONNIE & SCOTT CASE

PERSONAL and ATHLETIC DATA

* Number 25 *
Safety - 6'1" - 188 lbs.

BORN: Scott -- 5-17-62 in Oklahoma

HIGH SCHOOL: Scott -- Alva High School and Edmond High School in Oklahoma

COLLEGE: Northwestern Oklahoma Junior College and University of Oklahoma

CHILDREN: Kelsey, Kyler, and Kody

YEARS IN PROFESSIONAL FOOTBALL: 12th year

HONORS OR AWARDS: Scott's brand of hard-hitting football can be traced back to his days as a young prep in Alva, Oklahoma; attended Northeastern Oklahoma Junior College, where he made a name for himself through his All-America play; went on to pace the Big Eight and establish a school mark for interceptions in a season with eight (for 181 return yards and a touchdown) during his senior year at safety; originally a Falcons' second-round draft choice out of Oklahoma, where he played under Cowboys' Head Coach Barry Switzer; one of just six players to play 11-or-more games with Atlanta; played in 162 career games with the Falcons, fourth highest in club history; third on the Falcons' all-time interception list with 30; signed August 24, 1995, as a free agent with the Dallas Cowboys

TOP: Dixon Edwards in action against the Jets.

BOTTOM: Dixon -- Number 58 -- playing defense against the New York Giants (1994).

SECOLA & DIXON EDWARDS, III

PERSONAL DATA

BORN: *Dixon* -- 3-25-68 in Cincinnati, Ohio; *Secola* -- 1-18-68 in Flint, Michigan

HIGH SCHOOL: *Dixon* -- Aiken High School in Cincinnati

COLLEGE: *Dixon* -- Michigan State University (Building Construction Management); *Secola* -- Michigan State University (Communications / Broadcast Journalism)

FAVORITE TYPE OF MUSIC: *Dixon* -- Rap, rhythm and blues, and hip hop; *Secola* -- Rhythm and blues

FAVORITE FOOD: *Dixon* -- Soul food; *Secola* -- Italian

FAVORITE AUTHOR: *Dixon* -- Secola Edwards; *Secola* -- Stephen King

FAVORITE SPORTS HERO: *Dixon* -- "My dad"; *Secola* -- Husband Dixon

HOBBIES AND INTERESTS: *Dixon* -- Automobiles, music, carpentry, and auto body mechanics; *Secola* -- Tennis, reading, and shopping

CHILDREN AND AGES: Twins - Dixon Voldean, IV, and Taylor Sierra Lyn - 4 yrs.

Edwards in training camp in 1991.

DIXON VOLDEAN EDWARDS, III

ATHLETIC DATA

* Number 58 *
Linebacker - 6'1" - 225 lbs.

FIRST PLAYED ORGANIZED FOOTBALL: In the fifth grade as a guard and tackle in Little League

YEARS IN PROFESSIONAL FOOTBALL: 5th year

ENJOY MOST ABOUT BEING WITH THE DALLAS COWBOYS: The winning attitude among players and coaches

HONORS OR AWARDS: Earned All-District and team MVP honors as a tight end and defensive tackle in high school; first season at Michigan State (1989) as starting weakside linebacker, earned honorable mention All-America honors; shared the Spartans' Defensive Player of the Year award as a senior; selected with highest choice Dallas has used on a linebacker since 1984; moved into starting lineup in 1993 at strong linebacker -- made 12 special teams tackles to lead all offensive and defensive starters; in 1994, third on team with 104 tackles, passing his career high of 82 set in 1993, and also tenth with 9 special teams tackles; received game ball for four tackles, one tackle for a loss, one quarterback pressure, and one fumble recovery against the New York Giants in 1994; since taking over the strongside linebacker job in 1993, has accounted for 186 tackles; has played in 70 consecutive regular and postseason games; a big contributor on the Cowboys' special teams units, accounting for 46 special teams tackles during his career and finishing near the top of the Dallas' special teams tackle chart each season

Fleming family picture: Tracey, Cory, Cory Jr., and TaCoria (April, 1995.

TRACEY & CORY FLEMING

PERSONAL DATA

BORN: *Cory* -- 3-19-71 in Nashville, Tennessee; *Tracey* -- 11-9-70 in Nashville, Tennessee

HIGH SCHOOL: *Cory* -- Stratford High School in Nashville

COLLEGE: *Cory* -- University of Tennessee (Psychology); *Tracey* -- Aladdin Beauty College (Cosmetology)

WIFE'S OCCUPATION: Full-time student

FAVORITE TYPE OF MUSIC: *Cory* -- Rap, rhythm and blues, classical, reggae, and some jazz; *Tracey* -- Rhythm and blues, and rap

FAVORITE FOOD: *Cory* and *Tracey* -- Seafood

FAVORITE SPORTS HERO: *Cory* -- Magic Johnson; *Tracey* -- Husband Cory

HOBBIES AND INTERESTS: *Cory* -- Basketball and working with kids; *Tracey* -- Going shopping and being with family

CHILDREN AND AGES: TaCoria Lavon - 3-1/2 yrs.; and Cory Lamont, Jr. - 2 yrs.

HOW MET SPOUSE: In high school, where Tracey was a cheerleader and Cory played sports

LONG-RANGE CAREER GOAL: Recreational psychologist, and working with kids (community)

School picture of TaCoria and Cory, Jr. -- taken August 28, 1995.

CORY LAMONT FLEMING

ATHLETIC DATA

* Number 82 *
Wide Receiver - 6'1" - 216 lbs.

FIRST PLAYED ORGANIZED FOOTBALL: Six years old, as quarterback and safety for B & B "Bulldogs"

YEARS IN PROFESSIONAL FOOTBALL: 2nd year

GREATEST MOMENT IN SPORTS: Being selected in third round in 1994 NFL Draft

HONORS OR AWARDS: Earned All-State honors at Stratford High School in Nashville; as senior, passed for 860 yards and 6 touchdowns, while adding 400 yards and 11 scores on the ground; selected the state's best back by the Atlanta Touchdown Club; also earned honorable mention All-State honors in basketball as a junior, leading the state in rebounding with better than 15 boards per game; letters in track and field as a high jumper; played in every game as a sophomore at Tennessee, catching 14 passes for 170 yards and 5 touchdowns; as a junior, led team with 40 receptions for 490 yards and 2 touchdowns; as senior, was second on the team with 39 catches for 596 yards and set a school single-season record 11 touchdowns; Tennessee's career record holder with 18 touchdown receptions, finishing his career with 94 catches; All-SEC; signed with Dallas Cowboys on August 3, 1994, and earned a roster spot with his play in the preseason, recording four receptions for 55 yards; second on team in preseason 1995 with 14 receptions for 215 yards (also team high); recorded longest reception of preseason for Dallas with a 67-yard grab vs. Buffalo on July 29, 1995

TOP: Jason and Brill Garrett in St. Bart's in the Caribbean.

BOTTOM: Brill and Jason with friends, Peter Milanu, Tom Criqui, and Mike Engels, at a Cubs game.

BRILL ALDRIDGE & JASON GARRETT

PERSONAL DATA

BORN: *Jason* -- 3-28-66 in Abington, Pennsylvania; *Brill* -- 12-8-65 in Chicago, Illinois

HIGH SCHOOL: *Jason* -- University High School in Chagrin, Ohio

COLLEGE: *Jason* -- Princeton University (A.B. -- History); *Brill* -- Princeton University (A.B. -- Woodrow Wilson School) and Harvard University (J.D. -- Law School)

FAVORITE TYPE OF MUSIC: *Jason* -- Folk, soul, rock, and rhythm and blues; *Brill* -- All types

FAVORITE FOOD: *Jason* -- Pasta primevera with chicken in a pesto sauce; *Brill* -- Quesadillas

FAVORITE AUTHOR: *Jason* -- Ernest Hemingway; *Brill* -- F. Scott Fitzgerald

FAVORITE SPORTS HERO: *Jason* -- Brian Sipe; *Brill* -- Michael Jordan

HOBBIES AND INTERESTS: *Jason* and *Brill* -- Movie watching, skeeball, reading, traveling, and whack-a-mole

FITNESS AND DIET TIP: Do some sort of exercise every day -- use variety and do things you enjoy -- you'll keep coming back; and drink water -- you can never be too hydrated!

TOP: Jason on "Sparkplug" at NFL-NCHA Cutting in April, 1995.

BOTTOM: Jason with Bill Riddle, horse trainer, at 1995 NFL-NCHA Cutting.

JASON GARRETT

ATHLETIC DATA

* Number 17 *
Quarterback - 6'2" -- 195 lbs.

FIRST PLAYED ORGANIZED FOOTBALL: In second grade played center for the Meadowwood "Eagles"

YEARS IN PROFESSIONAL FOOTBALL: 3rd year

HONORS AND AWARDS: All-League safety and quarterback at University High School in Chagrin, Ohio; lettered in basketball and baseball, earning All-League honors in basketball; honorable mention All-America selection at Princeton as a senior; established NCAA Division 1-AA records for single-season completion percentage (68.2%) and lowest percentage of passes intercepted (1.0%) at Princeton; named the Ivy League Player of the Year in 1988; elevated to back-up duty as quarterback following final preseason game at Chicago in 1993; although third quarterback most of the season in 1994, Garrett will always be remembered for leading a spectacular late November victory -- although inactive for first ten games, saw his first action of the season against Washington, replacing Aikman and Peete, who were injured during the game, and finishing out the victory; in only second NFL start, led Dallas to a 42-31 come-from-behind victory against Green Bay with a club record 36 second-half points -- received a game ball from the coaches, earned NFC Offensive Player of the Week honors, and was named the NFL/Miller Lite Player of the Week for this victory; has become valuable as a Dallas back-up quarterback for last two seasons and will again, this year, provide Dallas valuable depth and experience at the number three quarterback spot behind Aikman and Wilson

The Haley family at Dallas Cowboys' Christmas Party at Valley Ranch on December 8, 1994 -- *(from left)* Karen, Princess (6 yrs.), CJ (4 yrs.), Brianna (11 months), and Charles.

KAREN & CHARLES HALEY

PERSONAL DATA

BORN: *Charles* -- 1-6-64 in Gladys, Virginia; *Karen* -- 10-10-64 in Richmond, Virginia

HIGH SCHOOL: *Charles* -- William Campbell High School in Naruna, Virginia

COLLEGE: *Charles* -- James Madison University (B.S. -- Social Science; *Karen* -- James Madison University (B.S. -- Public Administration and Political Science; M.P.A. - Public Administration)

FAVORITE TYPE OF MUSIC: *Charles* and *Karen* -- All types, especially rhythm and blues

FAVORITE FOOD: *Charles* -- Any type of Southern cooking; *Karen* -- All types, especially Mexican

FAVORITE AUTHOR: *Charles* -- All Black authors; *Karen* -- Alice Walker, Terry McMillan, Maya Angelou, Be Be Moore Campbell, and J. California Cooper

FAVORITE SPORTS HERO: *Charles* -- Muhammad Ali, Michael Jordan, and Joe Montana; *Karen* -- Michael Jordan

HOBBIES AND INTERESTS: *Charles* -- Playing cards and dominoes, motorcycle riding, and listening to music; *Karen* -- Reading books

CHILDREN AND AGES: Princess Kay - 7 yrs.; Charles, Jr. "CJ" - 5 yrs.; and Brianna - 1-1/2 yrs.

PETS: Four Doberman Pinchers: "Dallas" - "Buffy" - "Cody" - "Midnight"

FITNESS AND DIET TIP: No pain -- no gain

LONG-RANGE CAREER GOAL: Coaching, and to be self-employed

TOP: *(from left)* Princess, Karen, Charles (holding Brianna), and CJ -- at Christmas party at Valley Ranch in 1994.

BOTTOM: Singing Birthday Telegram for 31st birthday -- Charles Haley at home on January 6, 1995.

CHARLES LEWIS HALEY

ATHLETIC DATA

* Number 94 *
Defensive End - 6'5" - 255 lbs.

FIRST PLAYED ORGANIZED FOOTBALL: As linebacker at William Campbell High School in Virginia

YEARS IN PROFESSIONAL FOOTBALL: 10th year

ENJOY MOST ABOUT BEING WITH THE DALLAS COWBOYS: Young team with a bright future

HONORS OR AWARDS: Starred in football, basketball, and track at William Campbell High School in Naruna, Virginia; led team with 130-or-more tackles in each of final three seasons at James Madison University; one of NFL's premier pass rushers; in 1993, led Cowboys in quarterback pressures (28) for the second straight season, while missing a fair amount of playing time due to injuries; in NFC title game, accounted for 6 tackles, 3 sacks, 5 quarterback pressures, and 2 forced fumbles in 1993; in 2 games against Buffalo Bills (one was Super Bowl XXVIII), totaled 9 tackles, 9 quarterback pressures, 1 forced fumble, and half a sack; following off-season back surgery after Super Bowl XXVIII, enjoyed finest season (1994) as a Cowboy and one of his top years as a pro; a first-team All-Pro selection, earned his fourth career Pro Bowl trip -- first as a Cowboy; compiled second-highest career sack total for a single season with a team-leading 12.5 (fourth best in NFL); led Cowboys in quarterback pressures (52) for third straight year, while forcing more fumbles (3) than any other Dallas defender; one of NFL's most gifted pass rushers, is considered one of the major keys to Dallas finishing the 1992 and 1994 seasons with NFL's top-rated defensive unit; led his team in sacks in seven of his nine previous NFL seasons; has played on eight playoff teams in nine years -- his teams have been victorious in 14 of 18 postseason games; played in six of the last seven NFC Championship games and four of the last seven Super Bowls; owns four Super Bowl rings

George Hegamin -- the first player from North Carolina State to be drafted by Dallas since 1982.

GEORGE HEGAMIN

PERSONAL DATA

BORN: 2-14-73 in Camden, New Jersey

HIGH SCHOOL: Camden High School in New Jersey

COLLEGE: North Carolina State University (Business Management)

FAVORITE ACADEMIC SUBJECT: Business Management

FAVORITE TYPE OF MUSIC: Rhythm and blues

FAVORITE FOOD: Soul food

FAVORITE AUTHOR: Malcolm X

FAVORITE SPORTS HERO: Magic Johnson

HOBBIES AND INTERESTS: Swimming, reading, and listening to music

FITNESS AND DIET TIP: Eat to live; don't live to eat

LONG-RANGE CAREER GOAL: Plans to purchase an NFL team after playing career is over

Hegamin -- Number 69 -- at training camp in 1995.

GEORGE HEGAMIN

ATHLETIC DATA

* Number 69
Tackle - 6'7" - 338 lbs.

FIRST PLAYED ORGANIZED FOOTBALL: As a junior in Camden (New Jersey) High School

YEARS IN PROFESSIONAL FOOTBALL: 2nd year

HONORS OR AWARDS: Lettered in football at Camden High School; as a senior, named All-America honorable mention by "USA Today"; unanimous All-State first-team pick as a defensive lineman; redshirt freshman in 1992, earned Freshman All-America honors by "The Football News" and named to All-ACC second team; first player from North Carolina State to be drafted by the Dallas Cowboys since 1982; largest player selected in the 1994 NFL Draft; largest player on Cowboys' roster; backs up at both tackle and guard on offensive line; has earned the reputation as a dominating blocker

TOP: Brooke and Dale Hellestrae in summer of 1995.

BOTTOM: Kendyll Paige Hellestrae at four months old.

BROOKE & DALE HELLESTRAE

PERSONAL DATA

BORN: *Dale* -- 7-11-62 in Phoenix, Arizona; *Brooke* -- 11-28-63 in Phoenix, Arizona

HIGH SCHOOL: *Dale* -- Saguaro High School in Scottsdale, Arizona

COLLEGE: *Dale* -- Southern Methodist University (Physical Education); *Brooke* -- Phoenix College

FAVORITE TYPE OF MUSIC: *Dale* -- Country and western; *Brooke* -- Bits of everything

FAVORITE FOOD: *Dale* -- Steak, lobster, and Mexican; *Brooke* -- Ice cream

FAVORITE AUTHOR: Dale -- John Grisham; *Brooke* -- Evelyn Christenson, Gary Smalley, and Frank Peretti

FAVORITE SPORTS HERO: *Dale* -- Walt Frazier; *Brooke* -- Brooks Robinson ("I was named after him!")

HOBBIES AND INTERESTS: *Dale* -- Golf, basketball, softball, pool, and volleyball; *Brooke* -- Golf, racquetball, most outdoor sports, and singing

CHILDREN AND AGES: Hillary Royce - 3-1/2 yrs.; and Kendyll Paige - 10 months

FITNESS AND DIET TIP: Eat what you like (in moderation); make exercise part of your daily routine (like brushing your teeth); and drink plenty of water

LONG-RANGE CAREER GOAL: First goal -- coaching; and second -- expand "Cookies by Design"

Hillary Royce Hellestrae at three years old.

DALE ROBERT HELLESTRAE

ATHLETIC DATA

* Number 70 *
Guard/Center - 6'5" - 286 lbs.

FIRST PLAYED ORGANIZED FOOTBALL: As an eight-year-old, for the Boys' Club football team, the "Banditos"

YEARS IN PROFESSIONAL FOOTBALL: 11th year

ENJOY MOST ABOUT BEING WITH THE DALLAS COWBOYS: Being part of this team that has improved each year -- rewarded by going to two Super Bowls

HONORS AND AWARDS: All-State pick in football and basketball at Saguaro High School in Scottsdale, Arizona; four-year letterman and two-year starter at Southern Methodist University, earned All-Southwest Conference honors as a senior in 1984; participated in Cotton, Sun, and Aloha Bowls; handles all of the Dallas' deep-snapping chores on punts and placekicks, delivering snaps that have been consistently perfect for five straight seasons; since Dale's arrival, the Cowboys have not had a punt blocked or a snap fumbled in 393 regular-season punts, and they have not had a fumbled snap in 190 field goal attempts; has provided the Cowboys with a very dependable offensive lineman and deep snapper

TOP: Tammy, Chad, and Chase riding in the Colorado mountains of Tammy's home.

BOTTOM: Tammy and Chad *(on right)* with friends having a night out in Dallas (October, 1994).

TAMMY & CHAD HENNINGS

PERSONAL DATA

BORN: *Chad* -- 10-20-65 in Elberon, Iowa; *Tamara (Tammy)* -- 12-11-66 in Salida, Colorado

HIGH SCHOOL: *Chad* -- Brenton Community High School

COLLEGE: *Chad* -- United States Air Force Academy (B.S. -- Financial Management); *Tammy* -- Americana Beauty Academy (trade school)

FAVORITE TYPE OF MUSIC: *Chad* -- Old rock; *Tammy* -- Instrumental, country, and western

FAVORITE FOOD: *Chad* -- Pizza; *Tammy* -- Mexican

FAVORITE AUTHOR: *Chad* -- Tom Clancy and Frank Peretti; *Tammy* -- Anne Rice

HOBBIES AND INTERESTS: *Chad* -- Reading, watching movies, mountain biking, salt water fish tank, and public speaking; *Tammy* -- Golf, reading, being in the mountains, starting to mountain bike, and spending time with family

CHILDREN AND AGES: Chase Hoover - 2 yrs.

PETS: 140-gallon fish tank (salt water)

FITNESS AND DIET TIP: Never give fitness up -- always be doing something; and follow your head, not your stomach

LONG-RANGE CAREER GOAL: Buy a ranch and raise kids; to follow God's plan for us

Chad and Chase tubing in San Antonio over the 4th of July, 1995.

CHAD HENNINGS

ATHLETIC DATA

* Number 95 *
Defensive Tackle - 6'6" - 288 lbs.

FIRST PLAYED ORGANIZED FOOTBALL: As a quarterback in junior high school

YEARS IN PROFESSIONAL FOOTBALL: 4th year

ENJOY MOST ABOUT BEING WITH THE DALLAS COWBOYS: Being a part of a team that has a winning tradition

HONORS AND AWARDS: Two-time All-State football player and State-Champion wrestler in Brenton Community High School; in 1985, earned honorable mention All-America and second-team All-WAC honors as a sophomore; in 1986, earned first-team All-WAC recognition while named honorable mention All-America; two-time Academic All-America NCAA Scholarship Winner; Japan Bowl MVP; 1987 Western Athletic Conference Defensive Player of the Year honors; 1987 All-America and Outland Trophy Winner; finished 1993 season with 17 tackles and 5 quarterback pressures; in 1994, took advantage of extra playing time to set career highs (35 tackles, 7.5 sacks, and 27 quarterback pressures) -- his 7.5 sacks, second on the team, were most sacks by a Dallas defensive tackle since 1988; received game ball in the 1994 season opener, recording three tackles, three quarterback pressures, and his first NFL sack at Pittsburgh; received second game ball the next week vs. Houston; received another game ball for his two sack, two tackle, three quarterback pressure performance against Philadelphia -- also adding his first NFL fumble recovery against the Eagles; received another game ball when he had four tackles, 1.5 sacks, three quarterback pressures, and his first career forced fumble against the New York Giants; added four tackles and three quarterback pressures during the playoffs

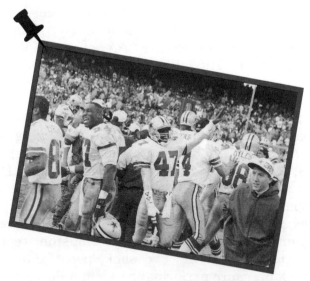

TOP: Clayton Holmes on a return run in 1994.

BOTTOM: Holmes saw action at both corner spots and as a punt and kickoff return man in 1994.

CLAYTON A. HOLMES

PERSONAL DATA

BORN: 8-23-69 in Florence, South Carolina

HIGH SCHOOL: Wilson High School in Florence

COLLEGE: Carson-Newman College (Management)

FAVORITE TYPE OF MUSIC: Soul, rap, and rhythm and blues

FAVORITE FOOD: New York strip steak

FAVORITE SPORTS HERO: Walter Payton

HOBBIES AND INTERESTS: Music, dancing, Nintendo, hanging with the guys, golf, and basketball

CHILDREN AND AGES: Dominique - 8 yrs.; and Kenya Briana - 2-1/2 yrs.

LONG-RANGE CAREER GOAL: Finish school, and own and manage a hotel

Clayton Holmes -- when playing for the Carson-Newman Eagles.

CLAYTON A. HOLMES

ATHLETIC DATA

* Number 47 *
Cornerback - 5'10" - 181 lbs.

FIRST PLAYED ORGANIZED FOOTBALL: When twelve years old as the quarterback and safety for the Tran-South "Volunteers"

YEARS IN PROFESSIONAL FOOTBALL: 4th year

HONORS OR AWARDS: Earned All-Conference honors as a quarterback and defensive back, and set the South Carolina state record in the long jump in high school; junior college All-America option quarterback at North Greenville, South Carolina; two-time NAIA All-America at cornerback at Carson-Newman; South Atlantic Conference's Defensive Player of the Year as a senior; drafted in the third round by Dallas in 1992, displayed his speed by running a 40-yard dash in Dallas' post-draft mini camp (4.23), the fastest 40-yard dash among both the Cowboys' rookies and veterans; sat out the entire 1993 season after tearing ligaments in right knee in a preseason game; saw action at both corner spots and as a punt and kickoff return man in 1994; selected to the Carson-Newman College Football Team of the Century in 1994; led team in punt returns with three for a six-yard average in 1995 preseason, and second on team in kickoff return average with a 27.7 average

Michael and Sandy *(standing)*; Sandy's mom, Jennie Pearl Blunt *(seated on left)* and Michael's mom, Stella Pearl Irvin *(seated on right)* -- out to dinner in Honolulu, Hawaii, at John Domins Seafood Restaurant.

SANDY & MICHAEL IRVIN

PERSONAL DATA

BORN: *Michael* -- 3-5-66 in Fort Lauderdale, Florida; *Sandy* -- 1-2-66 in Miami, Florida

HIGH SCHOOL: *Michael* -- St. Thomas Aquinas High School in Fort Lauderdale

COLLEGE: *Michael* -- University of Miami (Major - Business Management; Minor - Communications)

FAVORITE TYPE OF MUSIC: *Michael* -- Hip hop (educated rap); *Sandy* -- Luther Vandross

FAVORITE FOOD: *Michael* and *Sandy* -- Seafood

FAVORITE SPORTS HERO: *Sandy* -- Husband Michael

HOBBIES AND INTERESTS: *Michael* -- Playing video games; host of the "Michael Irvin Show" -- a weekly television show that runs throughout the football season; in each of the past two training camps, Michael has teamed up with Southwest Airlines to fly nearly 100 under-privileged children to Austin to spend a day with the Cowboys; *Sandy* -- Spending time with Michael, movies, and going out for dancing and dinner

CHILDREN AND AGES: Myesha Beyonca - 5-1/2 yrs.

Myesha and Sandy at football game in Texas Stadium.

MICHAEL JEROME IRVIN

ATHLETIC DATA

* Number 88 *
Wide Receiver - 6'2" - 205 lbs.

YEARS IN PROFESSIONAL FOOTBALL: 8th year

HONORS OR AWARDS: Earned All-State honors at St. Thomas Aquinas High School in Fort Lauderdale; a fine basketball player -- won several slam-dunk contests in the Florida area while in college; holds Miami career records for catches, receiving yards, and touchdown receptions; 11 touchdown catches in 1986 -- Hurricanes' record; involved in two of the Cowboys' three longest plays in 1990 -- giving Irvin four of Dallas' eight longest plays since 1988 -- other than quarterbacks, no other Cowboys' player has been involved in more than one of those big plays; in 1988, became first Cowboys' rookie wide receiver to start a season opener since Bob Hayes in 1965; in 1990, led Dallas in yards-per-catch and had the team's longest reception; in 1991, a career-best season with single season club record numbers for receptions and receiving yards, led NFC in catches, and led the NFL in yardage; in 1991 -- eclipsed Bob Hayes' club record for 100-yard receiving games with seven and earned consensus All-Pro recognition; named MVP of the Pro Bowl in first appearance in Hawaii; led Dallas in receptions and yardage for the fourth straight year; only Dallas receiver to be selected to four Pro Bowls (1991-1994); has 26 career 100-yard receiving games in regular season, tied for the Cowboys' all-time record; only player in Dallas history with four consecutive seasons with over 50+ receptions; has team-long streak of 67 games (74 including playoffs) with at least one reception, the second longest streak in club history; his career receiving average of 16.6 is fourth all-time in team history; third on team's all-time receiving list with 429 career catches; first Cowboys' player with four 75-catch seasons and has posted top four single-season reception totals in team history in past four years; has led or tied for team lead in receptions or receiving yards in 27 of the past 38 games

Jacque and John Jett in Dallas.

JACQUE & JOHN JETT

PERSONAL DATA

BORN: *John* -- 11-11-68 in Richmond, Virginia; *Jacque* -- 1-18-71 in Lenoir, North Carolina

HIGH SCHOOL: *John* -- Northumberland High School in Heathsville, Virginia

COLLEGE: *John* -- East Carolina University (B.S.B.A. -- Finance; *Jacque* -- East Carolina University (B.A. -- Economics)

WIFE'S OCCUPATION: Part-time sales representative

FAVORITE TYPE OF MUSIC: *John* -- Country (Garth Brooks and George Strait)

FAVORITE FOOD: *John* -- Grilled dolphin; *Jacque* -- Macaroni and cheese

FAVORITE SPORTS HERO: *John* -- Fred Lynn

HOBBIES AND INTERESTS: *John* and *Jacque* -- Fishing, water skiing, hunting, golf, and being outdoors; John supports the Children's Cancer Fund, participating in an annual fashion show and donating $100 for every one of his punts inside the 20-yard line

PETS: "Bugsy" and "Wyatt"

FITNESS AND DIET TIP: Exercise at least four times a week, and cut out the fat grams

LONG-RANGE CAREER GOAL: Go back to Virginia and run father's boat dealership when he retires

Jacque and John at John's sister's wedding.

JOHN JETT

ATHLETIC DATA

* Number 19 *
Punter - 6'0" - 184 lbs.

FIRST PLAYED ORGANIZED FOOTBALL: When a ten-year-old, the quarterback for the Fleeton "Eagles"

YEARS IN PROFESSIONAL FOOTBALL: 3rd year

HONORS OR AWARDS: Starred in football and baseball at Northumberland High School in Heathsville, Virginia; earned first-team All-State honors as an outfielder and pitcher; four-year letterman at East Carolina University; established as top punter in school history, setting a Pirates' career mark for punting average (40.1); honorable mention All-America (Sporting News) and second-team All-South Independent Selection in 1991; finished 1993 season ranked third in NVC in net punting average with a 37.7 mark; highest net punting average by a Dallas player since 1964; averaged better than 50 yards per punt in three games in 1993; closed a very successful rookie year with a 41.8 gross punting average; his efforts helped the Cowboys finish 1993 regular season ranked second in the NFL with an opponents' punt return average of just 5.3 yards; in 1994, Jett led the NFL in percentage of punts downed inside the 20 yard line (37.1%) and his 26 punts that landed inside the 20 were the third highest ever by a Dallas punter; received a game ball for efforts in Philadelphia -- hitting on five punts for a 49.2 yard average and all five of his punts were between 44 and 52 yards in length; has performed with poise of a seasoned veteran in each of first two pro seasons, being extremely consistent and productive; has not had a blocked punt in 142 regular season and playoff career attempts

Daryl and Fianceé Diane Krebs -- just happy to be together.

DARYL PETER (MOOSE) JOHNSTON

PERSONAL DATA

BORN: *Daryl* -- 2-10-66 in Youngstown, New York; *Diane Krebs* (Fiancée) -- 10-22-67 in Philadelphia, Pennsylvania

HIGH SCHOOL: *Daryl* -- Lewiston-Porter High School in Youngstown

COLLEGE: *Daryl* -- Syracuse University (B.A. -- Economics)

FIANCÉE'S OCCUPATION: Model

FAVORITE TYPE OF MUSIC: *Daryl* -- Alternative; *Diane* -- Classic rock, rhythm and blues, and classical

FAVORITE FOOD: *Daryl* -- Italian; *Diane* -- Vegetables, pasta, and dessert

FAVORITE AUTHOR: *Daryl* -- Tom Clancy; *Diane* -- Anne Rice

FAVORITE SPORTS HERO: *Daryl* -- Larry Csonka; *Diane* -- Daryl Johnston

HOBBIES AND INTERESTS: *Daryl* -- Jet skiing, snow skiing, golf, and spending time with Diane; hosted a weekly radio show on KRLD during the season, called "The Moose Call"; supports literacy groups in Texas and promotes helmet safety; *Diane* -- Going to movies and plays, reading, cooking . . . and especially walking with my fiancé

FITNESS AND DIET TIP: *Daryl* -- Nutrition is as important as exercise -- don't eat big meals late at night; *Diane* -- Fitness: cardiovascular exercise, weight training, and nutrition

TOP: Daryl and Mark Stepnoski about to conquer the most intense white water in the world.

BOTTOM: Johnston received Ed Block Courage Award in 1992, given to a player who demonstrates unusual courage in dealing with injuries.

DARYL PETER (MOOSE) JOHNSTON

ATHLETIC DATA

* Number 48 *
Fullback -- 6'2" -- 242 lbs.

FIRST PLAYED ORGANIZED FOOTBALL: In 1975, as a running back for the Lewiston-Porter "Chargers" -- 80-pound team

YEARS IN PROFESSIONAL FOOTBALL: 7th year

ENJOY MOST ABOUT BEING WITH THE DALLAS COWBOYS: Close friendships with teammates

HONORS OR AWARDS: Named Western New York Player of the Year while playing for Lewiston-Porter High School in Youngstown, New York, in 1983; graduated first in class of 290 students with a 4.0 grade -point average; All-America and All-East first-team pick in 1988; co-captain of the 1989 Syracuse Orangemen; All-Madden Team in 1992; selected for the Ed Block Courage Award in 1992 for demonstrating unusual courage in dealing with injuries; in 1993 -- first fullback selected to the Pro Bowl, earned All-Pro honors from "Sports Illustrated", and finished 5th in NFC in receptions among running backs; the Cowboys' lead blocker in the past five seasons; has never missed a game in his NFL career, playing in 106 straight, including playoffs; went to Pro Bowl again in 1995; long respected by his teammates for his contribution to the Dallas offense, is also garnering the admiration of players and coaches throughout the League with being chosen by the NFC as the Pro Bowl's selection of a fullback for two years in a row; successful 17-of-20 times he's run on third or fourth down for a first down during career; his 11 career touchdown catches are third highest active total on Cowboys' team; with 186 regular-season receptions and 1,483 yards, is second to Emmitt Smith among active Cowboys' running backs in receptions and receiving yards

TOP: Maneesha with sons, Isaiah and Cayleb, in front of the Luxor Hotel in Las Vegas (7-4-95).

BOTTOM: Jones family with Caleb's and Isaiah's maternal grandparents, "Nani and Papa," in Emerald City of MGM Grand Hotel in Vegas (7-4-95).

MANEESHA & ROBERT JONES

PERSONAL DATA

BORN: *Robert* -- 9-27-69 in Blackstone, Virginia; *Maneesha* -- 7-2-72 in York, Pennsylvania

HIGH SCHOOL: *Robert* -- Nottaway High School in Blackstone

COLLEGE: *Robert* -- East Carolina University (Criminal Justice); *Maneesha* -- West Virginia University, East Carolina University, and University of North Texas (Psychology)

WIFE'S OCCUPATION: Mother of two boys and student at University of North Texas

FAVORITE TYPE OF MUSIC: *Robert* -- Rhythm and blues, and rap; *Maneesha* -- Rhythm and blues, and gospel

FAVORITE FOOD: *Robert* -- Pork chops and chicken; *Maneesha* -- Shrimp and brownies

FAVORITE AUTHOR: *Robert* -- John Grisham; *Maneesha* -- James Dobson

FAVORITE SPORTS HERO: *Robert* -- Michael Jordan; *Maneesha* -- Husband Robert and Jeff Blake (brother; and quarterback for Cincinnati Bengals)

HOBBIES AND INTERESTS: *Robert* -- Golf, playing video games, remote control cars, and being with family; *Maneesha* -- Native American dancing, working out, watching football, reading the Bible, and attending Bible studies

CHILDREN AND AGES: Cayleb - 2 yrs.; and Isaiah - 5 months

FITNESS AND DIET TIP: Get in shape, lift hard, and stretch well -- to cut the fat off your body, cut it out of your diet!

LONG-RANGE CAREER GOAL: Hopefully, work in the ministry, and have many children!

TOP: Maneesha and Robert with friend, actress Kimberlin Brown ("*Sheila*" on "*The Bold and the Beautiful*") at Michael Jordan Celebrity Golf Classic on June 25, 1995.

BOTTOM: Robert Jones reclaimed the starting middle linebacker spot in 1994.

ROBERT LEE JONES

ATHLETIC DATA

* Number 55 *
Linebacker - 6'2" - 250 lbs.

FIRST PLAYED ORGANIZED FOOTBALL: In junior high for the Nottaway "Cougars" in Blackstone, Virginia

YEARS IN PROFESSIONAL FOOTBALL: 4th year

ENJOY MOST ABOUT BEING WITH THE DALLAS COWBOYS: Being associated with team chaplain and wife, John and Carol Weber

HONORS OR AWARDS: Four-year letterman at Nottaway High School, recording 120 tackles and led team to the 2A State Championship as a senior; unanimous first-team All-America in 1991 and finalist for the Dick Butkus Award, given annually to the nation's top collegiate linebacker, ending college career with 478 tackles; East-West Shrine Game; Defensive MVP of Peach Bowl (1991 ECU vs. NC State); first-round draft pick out of ECU ever; honor roll at ECU; NFC Defensive Rookie of the Year and All-Rookie Team in 1992; second leading tackler in 1992; Super Bowl Champ as a rookie; in 1993, first player with back-to-back double-digit tackle games since September, 1991; starting middle linebacker for Cowboys in 1994; started 1994 season with 9 tackles, earning a game ball; his efforts earned him "USA Today" All-Pro honors; received another game ball for leading team in tackles (11) and contributing two key goal-line stops in the final minute of victory over Philadelphia; received a game ball the next week, recording 13 tackles and helping limit the Cardinals running game to 2.9 yard average on 37 carries; received another game ball, recording a career-high 19 tackles, tying for the third most in Dallas history, at Philadelphia; Jones, starting in the middle, the Dallas Cowboys' defense finished the 1992 and 1994 seasons as the top-ranked defense in the NFL

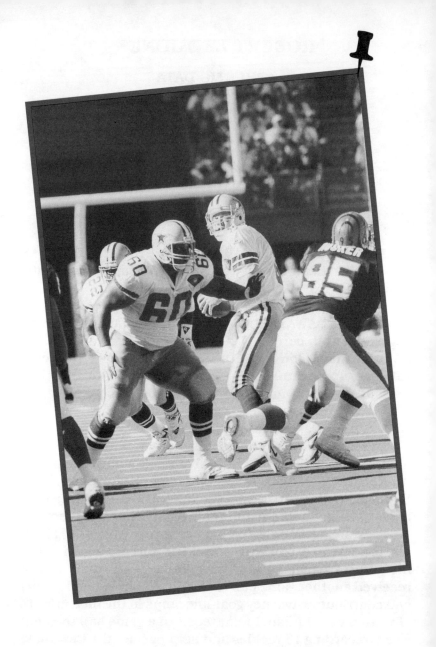

Derek Kennard -- playing in Cincinnati game in 1994.

DENISE & DEREK KENNARD

PERSONAL DATA

BORN: *Derek* -- 9-9-62 in San Mateo, California; *Denise* -- 2-3-62 in Bakersfield, California

HIGH SCHOOL: *Derek* -- Edison High School in Stockton, California

COLLEGE: *Derek* -- University of Nevada - Reno (Criminal Law); *Denise* -- Stockton's Private Business College

FAVORITE TYPE OF MUSIC: *Derek* and *Denise* -- Rap, rhythm and blues, and jazz

FAVORITE FOOD: *Derek* -- Cajun, seafood, and ribs; *Denise* -- Soul food and Mexican

FAVORITE AUTHOR: *Derek* -- John Grisham; *Denise* -- Terry McMillan

FAVORITE SPORTS HERO: *Derek* -- Muhammad Ali

HOBBIES AND INTERESTS: *Derek* -- Golf, fishing, and swimming; *Denise* -- Sewing, crafts, and shopping

CHILDREN AND AGES: Derek, Jr. - 13 yrs.; Denisha - 9 yrs.; and Devon Jay - 4 yrs.

FITNESS AND DIET TIP: Drink plenty of water (one gallon per day) and curb appetite

LONG-RANGE CAREER GOAL: Open up a group home for boys and be a counselor for juvenile delinquents

Kennard at training camp in Austin, 1995.

DEREK CRAIG KENNARD

ATHLETIC DATA

* Number 60 *
Guard - 6'3" - 333 lbs.

FIRST PLAYED ORGANIZED FOOTBALL: As nose guard for Southside "Vikings" in Stockton, California (Pop Warner)

YEARS IN PROFESSIONAL FOOTBALL: 10th year

HONORS OR AWARDS: All-America in high school; starred at Edison High School in Stockton; two-time All-Big Sky Conference selection and a Division 1-AA All-America as a senior at the University of Nevada - Reno in 1983; NFL honorable mention All-Pro at center in 1988; earned second-team All-Pro honors in 1992; signed as an unrestricted free agent by Dallas in April, 1994; signed with Dallas on August 3, 1995, and then left camp with a hip injury on August 4; started all 16 games for Dallas in 1994 at right guard; started 119 of 127 games over the past eight seasons with Cowboys, Saints, and Cardinals

TOP: Dallas Cowboys signed unrestricted free agent David Lang on April 27, 1995.

BOTTOM: Lang, understanding Dallas' offensive system, provides the Cowboys with an experienced back behind Daryl Johnston and Emmitt Smith.

DAVID LANG

PERSONAL and ATHLETIC DATA

* Number 38 *
Running Back - 5'11" - 210 lbs.

BORN: 3-28-68 in San Bernardino, California

HIGH SCHOOL: Eisenhower High School in Rialto, California

COLLEGE: Northern Arizona (Criminal Justice)

YEARS IN PROFESSIONAL FOOTBALL: 5th year

HOBBIES AND INTERESTS: Bowling, skiing, and horseback riding

HONORS OR AWARDS: All-League selection in football and anchored the 4 x 100 meter relay team that finished third at the California state finals, as a senior in high school; finished up career at Northern Arizona with a career-high 189 yards rushing, including a 70-yard touchdown, and 106 yards receiving, including a 80-yard touchdown; as a senior, led the Lumberjacks in rushing with 521 yards on 94 carries and in receiving with 41 catches for 477 yards; in 1994, led the Los Angeles Rams with 27 kickoff returns for 626 yards, good for a 23.2 yard average -- ninth best in the NFC; played mostly special teams in four seasons with the Rams; signed with the Dallas Cowboys on April 27, 1995, to help shore up Dallas special teams

CHILDREN AND AGES: Daivisha - 7 yrs.; and Derni - 3 yrs.

TOP: Leon Lett -- nicknamed "Big Cat" by teammates for his agility.

BOTTOM: Lett -- Number 78 -- in action against San Francisco, 1994.

LEON LETT

PERSONAL and ATHLETIC DATA

* Number 78 *
Defensive Tackle - 6'6" - 288 lbs.

BORN: 10-12-68 in Fairhope, Alabama

HIGH SCHOOL: Fairhope High School

COLLEGE: Emporia State University (Sociology)

YEARS IN PROFESSIONAL FOOTBALL: 5th year

FAVORITE TYPE OF MUSIC: Rhythm and blues

FAVORITE FOOD: Italian, especially lasagna

FAVORITE AUTHOR: Alex Haley

FAVORITE SPORTS HERO: Ed "Too Tall" Jones

CHILDREN AND AGES: Shanavia - 8 yrs.

HONORS OR AWARDS: Starred in football and basketball in high school; received honorable mention NAIA All-America, All-NAIA District 10, and All-CSIC honors in 1989; twice named District 10 Player of the Week as a junior at Emporia State; first person from Emporia State to make a Cowboys' roster; nicknamed "Big Cat" by teammates for his agility; led all defensive linemen in batted passes in 1992; finished 1992 tied for second on team with 19 quarterback pressures, including at least one pressure in final seven regular season games; in post season, tied for team lead with two tackles for losses and led team with three forced fumbles; established record for the longest fumble return in Super Bowl history -- 64 yards in fourth quarter with a Buffalo miscue; seeing action in only 11 games, led all defensive linemen in passes deflected for second straight season; despite being hobbled during 1993 season with a broken ankle, displayed tremendous athletic ability and versatility in moving along the defensive line to replace fallen teammates; started all 16 games and collected 68 tackles, topping his three-year career total in 1994; his 26 quarterback pressures were good for second on the team, helping him earn a spot as a starting defensive tackle for the NFC at Pro Bowl in 1994

Keri and Brock sharing a dance at their wedding in 1995.

KERI & BROCK MARION

PERSONAL DATA

BORN: *Brock* -- 6-11-70 in Wheeling, West Virginia; *Keri* -- 6-5-71 in Modesto, California

HIGH SCHOOL: *Brock* -- West High School in Bakersfield, California

COLLEGE: *Brock* -- University of Nevada (Architecture and Interior Design); *Keri* -- University of Nevada - Reno, and University of North Texas (English for Secondary Education)

WIFE'S OCCUPATION: Mother and student

FAVORITE TYPE OF MUSIC: *Brock* -- Rhythm and blues, rap, and jazz; *Keri* -- Classical (piano) and jazz

FAVORITE FOOD: *Brock* -- Pasta and seafood (crab legs); *Keri* -- Anything chocolate

FAVORITE AUTHOR: *Brock* -- Romantic poets (i.e., Keats, Shelly); *Keri* -- Shakespeare and most classical English literature authors

FAVORITE SPORTS HERO: *Brock* and *Keri* -- Michael Jordan

HOBBIES AND INTERESTS: *Brock* -- Fishing, listening to music, computers, and collecting jazz memorabilia; *Keri* -- Reading, gardening, and antique shopping

CHILDREN AND AGES: Briana Elise - 2 yrs.

PETS: Dog - "Sheba"

FITNESS AND DIET TIP: Eat three good meals a day

LONG-RANGE CAREER GOAL: Have own architectural firm

TOP: Briana Marion (almost 2 yrs.) after an evening swim in June, 1995.

BOTTOM: Brock and Briana - "Piggy-Back Rides".

BROCK MARION

ATHLETIC DATA

* Number 31 *
Safety - 6'0" - 190 lbs.

FIRST PLAYED ORGANIZED FOOTBALL: In the second grade

YEARS IN PROFESSIONAL FOOTBALL: 3rd year

HONORS OR AWARDS: Earned nine varsity letters in football, basketball, and track at West High School in Bakersfield, California; All-State selection as senior -- led State with 13 interceptions; three-time All-Conference selection, twice All-Big Sky, and once (first team) Big West; only the second player from Nevada-Reno ever chosen by the Dallas Cowboys; earned two awards for Special Teams Player of the Game during rookie year, finishing in the top three for special teams tackles in each of his first two seasons; recorded his first career sack, along with four tackles and a forced fumble, earning a game ball against the New York Giants in 1994; finished the 1994 regular season tied for third on the team with 23 special teams tackles, and was second among all non-starters with 29 defensive stops; having been a staple for the Cowboys' special teams units and providing good play in the "45" and nickel defenses, Marion will endeavor to make a name for himself in the Cowboys' defensive backfield in 1995

TOP: Russell Maryland is usually last player off field after each practice, taking extra time perfecting techniques with extra individual work.

BOTTOM: Maryland signs autographs at training camp, 1995.

ROSE & RUSSELL MARYLAND

PERSONAL and ATHLETIC DATA

* Number 67 *
Defensive Tackle - 6'1" - 279 lbs.

BORN: *Russell* -- 3-22-69 in Chicago, Illinois

HIGH SCHOOL: *Russell* -- Whitney Young School in Chicago

COLLEGE: *Russell* -- University of Miami (B.A. -- Psychology)

YEARS IN PROFESSIONAL FOOTBALL: 5th year

FIRST PLAYED ORGANIZED FOOTBALL: As a ninth grader for the Whitney Young "Dolphins" as offensive tackle and defensive end in 1981

FAVORITE TYPE OF MUSIC: *Russell* -- All types of good music -- especially rhythm and blues, and rap

FAVORITE FOOD: *Russell* -- Spaghetti

FAVORITE AUTHOR: *Russell* -- Alex Haley

FAVORITE SPORTS HERO: *Russell* -- Walter Payton

HOBBIES AND INTERESTS: *Russell* -- Listen to music; involved with inner-city Boy Scouts in Dallas, and very active in several charitable interests with the Russell Maryland Foundation in hometown of Chicago

HONORS OR AWARDS: Starred as two-way lineman in high school; played on two-time National Champions Miami team (1987 and 1989); two-time first-team All-America at Miami; winner of 1990 Outland Trophy; first player selected in 1991 NFL Draft; 1991 -- named NFL Rookie of the Year by Edelstein Pro Football Letter and earned All-Rookie honors from Pro Football Writers of America, "Pro Football Weekly", and "College & Pro Football Newsweekly"; 1993 -- selected to first Pro Bowl after just three seasons in NFL, and ranked second on team in tackles among defensive linemen, with 56 stops; started all 16 games in 1994, helping Cowboys earn the NFL's No. 1 overall defensive ranking; since 1991, combined total of forced fumbles (7) and fumbles recovered (5) is greater than any other Dallas player during that four-season span

McCormack at training camp in Austin, Texas (1995).

HURVIN McCORMACK

PERSONAL and ATHLETIC DATA

* Number 99 *
Defensive Tackle - 6'5" - 274 lbs.

BORN: 4-6-72 in Brooklyn, New York

HIGH SCHOOL: New Dorp High School in Brooklyn

COLLEGE: University of Indiana (Sports Management)

YEARS IN PROFESSIONAL FOOTBALL: 2nd year

FIRST PLAYED ORGANIZED FOOTBALL: Freshman year in high school as defensive end

FAVORITE TYPE OF MUSIC: Jazz, rap, rhythm and blues, and reggae

FAVORITE FOOD: West Indian and Italian

FAVORITE AUTHOR: John Grisham

FAVORITE SPORTS HERO: Michael Jordan

HOBBIES AND INTERESTS: Listening to music

HONORS OR AWARDS: All-City, All-District, and All-Conference selection during career at New Dorp High School; All-America honorable mention and All-Big 10 Conference second-team pick; voted by peers, in 1993, as team captain for Indiana; made team in 1994 as a rookie free agent defensive tackle; led all defensive linemen with 14 tackles and two sacks in 1995 preseason; moved to defensive end in 1995 during training camp

TOP: Godfrey Myles -- Number 98 -- an important member of the Cowboys' special teams units.

BOTTOM: Myles is equally adept at covering pass receivers out of the backfield or stopping the run.

JANICE & GODFREY MYLES

PERSONAL and ATHLETIC DATA

* Number 98 *
Linebacker - 6'1" - 242 lbs.

BORN: *Godfrey* -- 9-22-68 in Miami, Florida

HIGH SCHOOL: *Godfrey* -- Carol City High School in Miami

COLLEGE: *Godfrey* -- University of Florida (Sociology)

YEARS IN PROFESSIONAL FOOTBALL: 5th year

FIRST PLAYED ORGANIZED FOOTBALL: As a running back/quarterback for Little League (75 lbs.) in 1975

ENJOY MOST ABOUT BEING WITH THE DALLAS COWBOYS: Unity

FAVORITE TYPE OF MUSIC: *Godfrey* -- Rhythm and blues, and ballads

FAVORITE FOOD: *Godfrey* -- Chicken and yellow rice

FAVORITE SPORTS HERO: *Godfrey* -- Lawrence Taylor

HOBBIES AND INTERESTS: *Godfrey* -- Music

HONORS OR AWARDS: Earned second-team All-State honors in high school; selected to Florida's 35-Man Super Squad that met a team of Georgia Prep All-Stars in summer of 1987; named the "most underrated player in the country" by "The Sporting News" prior to his junior year; All-Southeastern Conference in 1990; honorable mention All-America pick (1989-1990); made name for himself as a hard-hitting special teamer, collecting 9 kick coverage tackles in 1992, and picked up first career interception in regular season finale; began 1993 season with a knee injury; spent 1994 backing up all three linebacker positions; starts 1995 at weakside linebacker

Nate, Dorothy, and Tré in Maui, Hawaii, in 1995.

DOROTHY & NATE NEWTON

PERSONAL DATA

BORN: Nathaniel (Nate) -- 12-20-61 in Orlando, Florida; Dorothy -- 12-20-61 in New Orleans, Louisiana

HIGH SCHOOL: Nate -- Jones High School in Orlando

COLLEGE: Nate -- Florida A & M University - Negro League (Physical Education); Dorothy -- University of Southwestern Louisiana - Lafayette (Accounting and Sociology)

WIFE'S OCCUPATION: Currently, attending TCJC, being certified to teach; and will be attending University of Arlington in the spring to complete a Master's Degree

FAVORITE TYPE OF MUSIC: Nate -- All music; Dorothy -- Rhythm and blues

FAVORITE FOOD: Nate -- Italian and French fries (potatoes of any kind); Dorothy -- Rice

FAVORITE AUTHOR: Nate -- Louis L'Amour; Dorothy -- Alex Haley

FAVORITE SPORTS HERO: Nate -- Mohammed Ali; Dorothy -- Husband Nate

HOBBIES AND INTERESTS: Nate -- Reading; Dorothy -- Playing competitive volleyball, softball, and reading love stories

HONORS OR AWARDS: Dorothy -- College on academic and volleyball scholarship

CHILDREN AND AGES: Nathaniel, III (Tre) - 6 yrs.

FITNESS AND DIET TIP: Nate -- Can nobody do what you can do for your own self

TOP: Tré, Dorothy, and Nate Newton at Benihana Restaurant in Honolulu, Hawaii (1995)

BOTTOM: Nathaniel Newton, III (5-1/2 yrs.) qualified in Texas State Tournament to attend Nationals in Los Angeles - the youngest to compete.

NATHANIEL (NATE) NEWTON, JR.

ATHLETIC DATA

* Number 61 *
Offensive Guard - 6'3" - 320 lbs.

FIRST PLAYED ORGANIZED FOOTBALL: Defensive end for the Windermere Recreation Department

YEARS IN PROFESSIONAL FOOTBALL: 10th year

ENJOY MOST ABOUT BEING WITH THE DALLAS COWBOYS: "Being able to provide for my family"

HONORS OR AWARDS: All-around athlete at Jones High School in Orlando, participating in football, basketball, wrestling and track (shot put); played on offensive and lines, winning four letters at Florida A & M; team captain and named All-Conference as a senior; named Cowboys' Most Valuable Offensive Player by "Pro Football Weekly" and the only offensive lineman to earn All-Pro votes from Associated Press in 1990; All-Pro, Pro Bowl, and Hall of Fame (Jones High School) in 1992; 1994 season marked the third straight Pro Bowl year for Nate; named All-Pro in 1994 by the Associated Press, "Sports Illustrated", "Pro Football Weekly/Pro Football Writers of America", "Football Digest" and "College & Pro Football Newsweekly"; selected the NFL Offensive Lineman of the Year by the NFL Alumni Association, while making his sixth straight All-Madden team selection; owner of two Super Bowl rings; possessing outstanding natural strength and quickness for a man of his size, has started 47 of the Cowboys last 48 regular season games at left guard; has started more regular season games on the offensive line (119) than any other current Cowboys' offensive player

TOP: Yvette had the opportunity to show her first 3-year-old cutting horse. Here she is showing "Lenaetta" (now 4 yrs.) in the Summer Cutting Spectacular in Fort Worth *(Courtesy of Jett Photography, Ft. Worth)*.

BOTTOM: Jay's most recent challenge on horseback was in May, 1995, at the Non-Pro in Oklahoma City, where he showed "Dr. Henry" without a bridle *(Courtesy of Jett Photography, Ft. Worth)*.

YVETTE & JAY NOVACEK

PERSONAL DATA

BORN: *Jay* -- 10-24-62 in Martin, South Dakota; *Yvette* -- 5-5-63 in Cozad, Nebraska

HIGH SCHOOL: *Jay* -- Gothenburg High School in Nebraska

COLLEGE: *Jay* -- University of Wyoming (Industrial Arts); *Yvette* -- University of Nebraska - Lincoln (B.S. -- Agricultural Economics)

FAVORITE TYPE OF MUSIC: *Jay* and *Yvette* -- Country

FAVORITE FOOD: *Jay* -- Wild game; *Yvette* -- Desserts

FAVORITE AUTHOR: *Jay* -- Louis L'Amour; *Yvette* -- John Grisham

FAVORITE SPORTS HERO: *Jay* -- Mike Beers (team roper); *Yvette* -- Phil Rapp (non-professional cutter)

HOBBIES AND INTERESTS: *Jay* -- Hunting and cutting horses; hosts two one-week football camps for youth (8-18) at Commerce, Texas, during the off-season; donates his time to Happy Hill Farm, Ducks Unlimited, Game Conservation international, and Rocky Mountain Elk Foundation; *Yvette* -- Cutting horses, baking desserts, and gives time and support to Happy Hill Farm; both Novaceks are members of Sanger Evening Lion's Club and Krum United Methodist Church

PETS: Horses - "Sackett", "Lady Blue", "Lenaetta", "Cola Doc", and "War Lena Drew"; Dogs - "Marlow", "Teal", and "Crockett"; and Cats -- "Chaps" and "Spurs"

FITNESS AND DIET TIP: Stretching is essential, and drink lots of water

LONG-RANGE CAREER GOALS: Return to their ranch in North Platte, Nebraska

TOP: Jay Novacek on "Dr. Henry" -- after their successful "bridleless" debut!

BOTTOM: Daryl Johnston, Troy Aikman, and Jay Novacek at a party, hosted by Mark and Pono Tuinei, in Hawaii during the 1995 Pro Bowl.

JAY MCKINLEY NOVACEK

ATHLETIC DATA

* Number 84 *
Tight End -- 6'4" - 235 lbs.

FIRST PLAYED ORGANIZED FOOTBALL: In the seventh grade for the Gothenburg "Swedes" Junior High School team in Nebraska

YEARS IN PROFESSIONAL FOOTBALL: 11th year

HONORS OR AWARDS: All-State quarterback at Gothenburg High School; University of Wyoming record holder in decathlon and pole vault; won Western Atlantic Conference Championship in decathlon in 1984; competed in decathlon at 1984 U. S. Olympic Trails; All-America at University of Wyoming; won team event in NFL-NCHA Celebrity Cutting; in 1994, selected to Pro Bowl for 4th straight season -- only tight end in club history; won 1993 NFL Alumni Tight End of the Year Award; selected, in 1995, to John Madden/Pat Summerall "All-Time Dallas Cowboys Team"; has caught more passes (277) than any other NFL tight end; can become first tight end, and only the third player in club history, to record four seasons with 50-or-more receptions; his 360 career receptions place him second among active Cowboys in career NFL catches; serves as the holder for field goals and extra points by Dallas kickers; since 1990, has 76 third or fourth-down catches for first downs, including 15 in 1994 to finish second among Cowboys' pass catchers; since coming to Dallas five seasons ago, only three NFL tight ends have more yards receiving (2,871); enters 1995 season with four 100-yard receiving games as a Cowboy (six in the NFL), --tied with Cosbie for the Dallas career record by a tight end, and should pass Cosbie in the 1995 season

Deion Sanders, with wife, Carolyn, after signing with the Cowboys
-- at a news conference in Dallas in September, 1995.

CAROLYN & DEION SANDERS

PERSONAL DATA

BORN: *Deion* -- 8-9-65 in Fort Myers, Florida; *Carolyn* -- 4-16-65 in San Antonio, Texas

HIGH SCHOOL: *Deion* -- North Fort Myers High School

COLLEGE: *Deion* -- Florida State University; *Carolyn* -- Florida A & M University (Psychology)

FAVORITE ACADEMIC SUBJECT: *Deion* -- English; *Carolyn* -- Math

WIFE'S OCCUPATION: Television and Film Producer -- weekly show on Black Entertainment Network

FAVORITE TYPE OF MUSIC: *Deion* and *Carolyn* -- Country

FAVORITE FOOD: *Deion* -- Soul food; *Carolyn* -- Shrimp

FAVORITE AUTHOR: *Carolyn* -- Terry McMillan and Jackie Collins

HOBBIES AND INTERESTS: *Deion* -- Fishing; *Carolyn* -- Reading and jogging

HOW YOU MET SPOUSE: Met in college

CHILDREN AND AGES: Deiondra -- 5yrs.; Deion, Jr. -- 2yrs.

TOP: Deion draws a crowd at Washington Redskins game in 1995.

BOTTOM: On the sideline at Washington Redskins game.

DEION LUWYNN "PRIME TIME" SANDERS

ATHLETIC DATA

* Number 21 *
Cornerback - 6'0" - 190 lbs.

FIRST PLAYED ORGANIZED FOOTBALL: For the "Rebels" in Fort Myers, Florida -- a national championship Pop Warner team

YEARS IN PRO FOOTBALL: 7th year

HONORS OR AWARDS: In high school, he acquired "Prime Time" nickname after scoring 36 points in a basketball game in his junior year; named Metro Conference's MVP for winning the individual 100- and 200-meter crowns in his first season of track; named two-time All-America and received Jim Thorpe Award as the best defensive back in collegiate game following his senior season; set FSU career records with 287 interception return yards (14 interceptions) and 1,429 punt return yards; played on teams that won four Bowl games during collegiate career; a member of Seminole's College World Series baseball team as a center fielder; selected by Atlanta Falcons in the first round of 1989 Draft; only athlete in modern history to score an NFL touchdown and hit a major league home run in the same week -- with the Falcons and New York Yankees in 1989; after Pro Bowl starting season in 1991, followed the next year by becoming leading Pro Bowl vote-getter at both cornerback and kickoff returner; 1992 season included racing 99 yards for a TD off a kickoff return the first time he touched the ball at Washington, leading NFL in KOR average at 26.7 and a total of 11 plays of 30-or-more yards; in 1993, played 11 games for Atlanta and led NFC with seven interceptions; NFL Defensive Player of the Year in 1994, setting NFL record with two interception returns of 90-or-more yards for touchdowns in the same season with the San Francisco 49ers; in 1991, opened season in Atlanta, becoming the first player to play baseball and football on the same field since 1945; signed a seven-year contract with the Dallas Cowboys in September, 1995

TOP: Brenda, Jim, and Ashlynne -- visiting friends in Plano, Texas.

BOTTOM: Jim and Ashlynne, after Jim let her get "creative" at the dinner table.

BRENDA & JIM SCHWANTZ

PERSONAL DATA

BORN: *Jim* -- 1-23-70 in Arlington Heights, Illinois; *Brenda* -- 4-14-71 in Arlington Heights, Illinois

HIGH SCHOOL: *Jim* -- William Fremd High School in Chicago, Illinois

COLLEGE: *Jim* -- Purdue University (B.A.); *Brenda* -- Purdue University (B.A. -- Sport Science; B.A. -- Health Promotion)

FAVORITE TYPE OF MUSIC: *Jim* and *Brenda* -- Country

FAVORITE FOOD: *Jim* and *Brenda* -- Italian

FAVORITE AUTHOR: *Jim* -- Michael Crichton; *Brenda* -- Dean R. Koontz

FAVORITE SPORTS HERO: *Jim* -- Walter Payton, Michael Jordan, and Mike Singletary; *Brenda* -- Husband Jim; and Amy Koopman, olympic gymnast and friend

HOBBIES AND INTERESTS: *Jim* -- Golf; *Brenda* -- Reading and jogging

CHILDREN AND AGES: Ashlynne Marie - 1 yr.

PETS: Three-year-old Chocolate Lab - "Cody"

FITNESS AND DIET TIP: Change up your workout periodically, and stay away from fast foods

LONG-RANGE CAREER GOAL: Coaching (high school level) and teaching

TOP: Ashlynne -- giving Cody a kiss.

BOTTOM: Jim's aggressive style allows him to make plays all over the field.

JAMES WILLIAM SCHWANTZ

ATHLETIC DATA

* Number 52 *
Linebacker - 6'2" - 232 lbs.

FIRST PLAYED ORGANIZED FOOTBALL: In freshman year in high school as tight end for the Vikings

YEARS IN PROFESSIONAL FOOTBALL: 2nd year

ENJOY MOST ABOUT BEING WITH THE DALLAS COWBOYS: Camaraderie with all the players

HONORS OR AWARDS: Selected the top defensive player in northwest Chicago by coaches after senior year at William Fremd High School; batted .501 as a sophomore on the baseball team and started on the basketball team; Purdue's MVP with 143 tackles and 12 tackles for a loss, as a senior in 1991; earned Big-Ten Defensive Player of the Week honors vs. Northwestern, when he returned a 66-yard interception for a touchdown; recorded 83 tackles as a junior; finished second in the conference with 10 sacks and had a career-best 16 tackles against Notre Dame as a sophomore; acquired by Dallas in a trade with Chicago in 1994; finished regular season with four defensive tackles and five special teams tackles in 1994; plays all three linebacker positions and provides the Cowboys with a reserve linebacker and also a quality special teams player; his aggressive style allows him to make plays all over the field

TOP: Emmitt Smith -- Super Bowl XXVIII MVP.

MIDDLE: Emmitt in pre-season, 1995.

BOTTOM: All-time great running back (#22) Emmitt Smith.

EMMITT J. SMITH, III

PERSONAL DATA

BORN: 5-15-69 in Pensacola, Florida

HIGH SCHOOL: Escambia (Florida) High School

COLLEGE: University of Florida (Therapeutic Recreation)

FAVORITE TYPE OF MUSIC: Rhythm and blues

FAVORITE FOOD: Barbecue ribs and chicken

FAVORITE AUTHOR: Alex Haley

FAVORITE SPORTS HERO: Tony Dorsett, Walter Payton, and Rocky Blier

HOBBIES AND INTERESTS: Golf, fishing, and dominos; in 1992, started Emmitt Smith Charity Golf Tournament - - played each March in Pensacola, with money going to help numerous groups in Pensacola area; a Miller Lite NFL Player of the Year finalist in 1991, 1992, and 1994 -- and the 1993 winner, donating all money received through the awards to the Sickle Cell Anemia Foundation; works with the Salvation Army, American Lung Association, the Battered and Abused Children's Foundation, and B.A.D. (Boxers against Drugs); makes speaking engagements at schools in the Dallas/Fort Worth area and in Pensacola; in 1994, a celebrity 25th birthday party was held for Emmitt with proceeds from a fundraising auction given to the "I Have a Dream" Foundation; Emmitt's mother, Mary - father, Emmitt - and sister, Marsha -- head up Emmitt, Inc., a marketing and promotions company that handles Smith's merchandising efforts

Emmitt Smith -- the first Dallas offensive player chosen to start four straight Pro Bowls.

EMMITT J. SMITH, III

ATHLETIC DATA

* Number 22 *
Running Back - 5'9" - 209 lbs.

YEARS IN PROFESSIONAL FOOTBALL: 6th year

HONORS OR AWARDS: Consensus All-America running back and Prep Play-of-the-Year by "Parade Magazine" and "USA Today" as a senior at Escambia (Florida) High School; posted third highest career rushing and scoring totals in national high school history with 8.804 yards and 106 touchdowns; All-America and three-time All-Southeastern Conference selection at Florida, establishing 58 school records in 3 seasons, including career-rushing mark of 3,928 yards; surpassed the 1,000-yard rushing mark in 7th game, earlier than any player in college football history; became second freshman to finish in Top 10 in Heisman Trophy balloting; in 1989, set school single-game rushing mark with 316 yards on way to school-record 1,599 yards rushing for the season; in 3 seasons, became 5th leading all-time rusher in SEC history - leading Gators in receiving in two-of-three seasons; started team-high 52 straight games, including playoffs (1990); earned consensus first-team All-Pro honors and All-NFC from UPI and "Football News"; joined Jimmy Johnson (1990) and Jerry Jones (1991) as recipients of "Big D" award from Dallas All-Sports Association (1992); led NFL in rushing in 1991 - becoming first Cowboy to lead League in rushing; became youngest player in NFL history and 28th overall to rush for over 1,500 yards in a season; in 1992, became 9th NFL player to win consecutive rushing titles - 1st since 1983-'84 - set new Dallas rushing record with 1,713 yards while leading NFL -- setting new Cowboys' standards for rushing touchdowns (18) and total touchdowns (19); became first player to win rushing title and Super Bowl in same season; posted 10th best rushing season in NFL history; first NFL player, since 1984-'85, with consecutive 1,500-yard rushing seasons; first player in team history with 3 straight seasons with 10-or-more rushing touchdowns; 2,048 yards from scrimmage set new Dallas record, led NFC, and second in NFL; in 1992, established Dallas mark for rushing attempts with 373, and rushing-receiving attempts from scrimmage with 432; became first Cowboy player to rush for 100 yards in a Super Bowl; some of 1993 honors and awards - Associated Press, "The Sporting News", Pro Football Writers of America, Miller Lite, the ESPN "ESPY" Awards, "Pro Football Weekly" and "Pro Football Digest" - 1993 NFL-MVP; United Press International, "Pro Football Weekly", and "College and Pro Football Newsweekly" - NFL Offensive Player of the Year; Bert Bell Award recipient from Maxwell Club as Player of the Year; consensus All-Pro; NFL Alumni Running Back of the Year; Super Bowl XXVIII MVP; only fourth player to win three straight rushing titles - and first since Earl Campbell in 1978-'80; first Dallas offensive player to start four straight Pro Bowls since Randy White in 1981-'83; joins Mel Renfro as only other player in team history to make Pro Bowl in his first five seasons in the NFL; with 22 touchdowns in 1994, now has 75 touchdowns through five seasons, fastest anyone in League history has reached that mark; only player in NFL history with four straight seasons with over 1,400 yards rushing; joined Jim Brown in 1994 as only players with five straight 10-touchdown season to start their career -- with 22 touchdown season in 1994, now has 75 touchdowns through five seasons, the fastest anyone in League history has reached that mark

TOP: Kevin Smith -- one of the NFL's most productive cornerbacks.

BOTTOM: Dallas Cowboys' first pick in 1992 NFL Draft, Kevin started in Super Bowl XXVII as a 22-year-old rookie.

KEVIN REY SMITH

PERSONAL and ATHLETIC DATA

* Number 26 *
Cornerback - 5'11" - 184 lbs.

BORN: 4-7-70 in Orange, Texas

HIGH SCHOOL: West Orange Stark High School

COLLEGE: Texas A & M (Recreation, Parks, and Tourism)

YEARS IN PROFESSIONAL FOOTBALL: 4th year

HONORS OR AWARDS: Earned second-team All-State honors, leading West Orange High School team to 15-0 record and a second consecutive Texas 4-A State Championship; big part of Aggies squad that compiled a 27-3-1 record, including 1991 SWC Title; played in three bowl games during college career; scored 6 special teams/defensive touchdowns in four years at A & M; set SWC record for career interceptions with 20, tied conference mark for career touchdowns on interceptions with 3, and set Texas A & M career records for interceptions yards (289) and passes defensed (32); started 38 straight games to end collegiate career; cornerstone of Aggies' secondary -- named the best in the country by "The Sporting News" prior to the season, with the Aggies leading the nation in defense and finishing second in the country in pass defense in 1991; semifinalist for Jim Thorpe Award; earned consensus All-America honors in 1991; third straight year -- All-SWC recognition in 1991; played in Japan Bowl and East-West Shrine Game following senior year; in 1990 earned SWC Defensive Player of the Week mention; picked off 9 passes -- second most in a season in Texas A & M history -- to lead SWC and finish fourth in nation; Cowboys' first pick in 1992 Draft -- selected with highest choice ever used on a defensive back from Texas A & M; first Aggie player drafted by Dallas since 1985; has 4.5 speed and big play ability; one of two Cowboys' rookies starting on Dallas' defensive unit in Super Bowl XXVII; 1992 -- youngest player on roster at age 21, and collected a career-high 8 tackles (7 solos) while returning fumble recovery 11 yards; led Cowboys in interceptions (6) in 1993; tied for second in NFC in interceptions, while finishing seventh overall in NFL; team's leader in passes defensed with 13, and tied for team lead in forced fumbles with 3; became first Cowboys' defender, since 1990, to be named NFC Defensive Player of the Week; in 1994, for second straight year, Cowboys' team leader in passes defensed with a career-high 17, and seventh on team in total tackles with 71; beginning 1995 season, had 38 consecutive regular season starts; over last two seasons, has averaged 80 tackles, 15 passes defensed, and 4 interceptions per year

Ron Stone, offensive lineman from Boston College, shows
potential to be an outstanding lineman in the NFL.

RON STONE

PERSONAL and ATHLETIC DATA

* Number 65 *
Offensive Lineman - 6'5" - 309 lbs.

BORN: 7-20-71

HIGH SCHOOL: West Roxbury (Massachusetts) High School

COLLEGE: Boston College (Sociology)

YEARS IN PROFESSIONAL FOOTBALL: 2nd year

HOBBIES AND INTERESTS: Spent the summer of 1992 working with inner-city youth in the Big East Conference's "Athletes Care" program

HONORS OR AWARDS: Served as team captain and blocked three punts in senior year of high school at West Roxbury; All-America and All-Big East first-team selection in 1992; only Boston College player selected in the 1993 Draft; though Stone saw most of his action in 1994 on field goal and extra point attempts, he did receive a significant amount of playing time all along the offensive line, usually due to an injured teammate; has made considerable strides while playing along side of Pro Bowlers Erik Williams, Mark Tuinei, and Nate Newton; first Golden Eagles' offensive lineman to be drafted by the Dallas Cowboys since 1988

TOP: Tasha (seven months pregnant) and Tony in Lake Tahoe, Nevada.

BOTTOM: Tony's other favorite girl -- "Midnight Tolbert".

TASHA & TONY TOLBERT

PERSONAL DATA

BORN: *Tony* -- 12-29-67 in Englewood, New Jersey; *Satasha (Tasha)* -- 3-29-68 in Germany

HIGH SCHOOL: *Tony* -- Dwight Morrow High School in Englewood

COLLEGE: *Tony* -- University of Texas - El Paso (B.S. -- Criminal Justice); *Tasha* -- University of Texas - El Paso (B.S. -- Biology)

FAVORITE TYPE OF MUSIC: *Tony* -- Rhythm and blues, and rap; *Tasha* -- Rhythm and blues, and gospel

FAVORITE FOOD: *Tony* and *Tasha* -- Italian and soul food

FAVORITE AUTHOR: *Tony* -- Alex Haley; *Tasha* -- Terry McMillan and Frank Peretti

FAVORITE SPORTS HERO: *Tony* -- Muhammad Ali

HOBBIES AND INTERESTS: *Tony* -- Buying music; *Tasha* -- Reading and learning to cook low-fat meals

CHILDREN AND AGES: Anthony Lewis Tolbert, Jr. - expected arrival in October, 1995

PETS: Chow-Shepherd mix - "Midnight Tolbert"

FITNESS AND DIET TIP: Watch what you eat . . . and keep moving

LONG-RANGE CAREER GOALS: *Tony* -- Make my wife go to work after I retire! *Tasha* -- Change my husband's mind!!

Tony and Tasha Tolbert -- after church on Easter Sunday, 1995.

TONY LEWIS TOLBERT

ATHLETIC DATA

* Number 92 *
Defensive End - 6'6" - 263 lbs.

FIRST PLAYED ORGANIZED FOOTBALL: In the sixth grade played defensive tackle for Englewood County team

YEARS IN PROFESSIONAL FOOTBALL: 7th year

ENJOY MOST ABOUT BEING WITH THE DALLAS COWBOYS: Being around the guys!

HONORS OR AWARDS: Earned All-Conference recognition at Dwight Morrow High School in Englewood, New Jersey; in 1988, earned All-Western Athletic Conference and honorable mention All-America honors -- leading the Miners in sacks and tackles for a loss; since 1990, piled up more quarterback sacks (41.5) than any other Dallas' defender; only Dallas' defensive player who has started every Cowboys' game -- 74 regular season and post-season outings -- since the beginning of the 1991 season; registered single season, career-high figures for solo tackles (57), total tackles (89) and tackles for lost yardage (7 for minus 15 yards); in 1994, his 11 tackles and two sacks at Philadelphia earned Tony a game ball as the Cowboys clinched the NFC Easter Division title; also picked up game balls vs. Washington and the Giants; recognized as one of the NFL's premier run-stopping defensive ends, has also been the Dallas Cowboys' top tackler among defensive linemen in each of the past four seasons, averaging 83.3 tackles per year; Tolbert's physical size and strength have increased in each of his six years in the League -- matching his steady rise in productivity on the field

Greg Tremble -- playing in 1995 preseason game.

GREG TREMBLE

PERSONAL and ATHLETIC DATA

* Number 27 *
Safety - 5'11" - 188 lbs.

BORN: 4-16-72 in Warner Robbins, Georgia

HIGH SCHOOL: Warner Robbins High School

COLLEGE: Northeast Oklahoma Junior College and University of Georgia

YEARS IN PROFESSIONAL FOOTBALL: 1st year

HONORS OR AWARDS: Two-year starter, played safety and returned punts for Warner Robbins High School in Georgia; attended Northeast Oklahoma Junior College, starting 10 of 14 games and leading the team in passes defensed with 16 while making 46 stops (25 solo), causing two fumbles - recovering one, and grabbing two interceptions - returning one for a touchdown; also led NOJC in punt returns with 15 for 227 yards (15.1 average); transferred to University of Georgia and moved from cornerback to free safety; as a senior, led Bulldogs in interceptions with three; started 22 games during his two-year career with Georgia and totaled 182 tackles (118 solo), six interceptions, 12 passes defensed, and three fumble recoveries; spent 1994 training camp with the Cleveland Browns; first season with the Dallas Cowboys -- signed as a free agent on March 9, 1995; led Dallas in tackles in 1995 preseason with 35

Mark and Pono Tuinei (Christmas, 1994).

PONO & MARK (TUI) TUINEI

PERSONAL DATA

BORN: *Mark* -- 3-31-60 in Oceanside, California; *Ponolani* (*Pono*) -- 2-25-   in Honolulu, Hawaii

HIGH SCHOOL: *Mark* -- Punahou High School in Honolulu

COLLEGE: *Mark* -- University of California - Los Angeles and University of Hawaii; *Pono* -- Santa Ana College (Liberal Arts)

WIFE'S OCCUPATION: Volleyball coach at Trinity Christian Academy (freshman girls); partner in business in Hawaii, titled Kidsports -- opening in mid-October in the Windward Mall, an edutainment center for children

FAVORITE TYPE OF MUSIC: *Mark* -- All types; *Pono* -- Hawaiian, jazz, and oldies

FAVORITE FOOD: *Mark* -- Hawaiian plate lunch; *Pono* -- Laulau (authentic Hawaiian dish) and poi

FAVORITE SPORTS HERO: *Mark* -- Muhammad Ali

HOBBIES AND INTERESTS: *Mark* -- Playing bass guitar, card games, and golf; *Pono* -- Music, sport coaching, talk radio, and making new friends

HONORS OR AWARDS: *Pono* -- Voted MVP by husband for contributions and support over the years

FITNESS AND DIET TIP: Drink lots of water daily (body weight divided by 2 in ounces, should suffice); eat lots of fiber and vegetables

LONG-RANGE CAREER GOAL: Be successful in business ventures

Taking time out at Kidsports, an edutainment center for children
opening in Hawaii in November, 1995.

MARK PULEMAU (TUI) TUINEI

ATHLETIC DATA

* Number 71 *
Tackle - 6'5" - 305 lbs.

FIRST PLAYED ORGANIZED FOOTBALL: In the ninth grade played defensive end for Punahou High School

YEARS IN PROFESSIONAL FOOTBALL: 13th year

ENJOY MOST ABOUT BEING WITH THE DALLAS COWBOYS: Meeting fans -- especially the children -- and all the friends and business acquaintances made through different events held for the team -- we will cherish the moments through all our lives

HONORS OR AWARDS: Starred at Punahou High School; Hawaii Prep Lineman of the Year as a senior; state shot put champion; all-star basketball player; defensive lineman turned offensive lineman, six years ago -- one of the only players to play both offense and defense in a NFL game; has played in more NFL games than any other Cowboys' offensive player; started all 13 games he played in 1990; started 15 of the 16 regular season games in 1992; started all 19 games during the 1993 season, including the postseason; in 1994, started 17 of 18 games of the season, including playoffs; received special recognition in Cowboys' 42-31 win over the Packers in which his blocking helped Dallas amass 436 yards of total offense; also received game balls in Cowboys' victory over New Orleans and in playoff win over Green Bay; has played in more NFL games (170) than any other Cowboys' offensive player, starting 54 games over the past three seasons; selected to NFC Pro Bowl squad in 1994 for first time; Offensive MVP by the NFL Alumni Dallas Chapter; tied with Bill Bates, Tuinei has longest current tenure with Dallas (11 years)

One of the biggest of Dallas' big men in the offensive front, Erik
Williams is a cornerstone on an offensive line that is one of the
largest in the history of the NFL.

ERIK GEORGE WILLIAMS

PERSONAL DATA

BORN: 9-7-68 in Philadelphia, Pennsylvania

HIGH SCHOOL: John Bartram High School in Philadelphia

COLLEGE: Central State University - Ohio (Physical Education)

FAVORITE TYPE OF MUSIC: Rhythm and blues, and jazz

FAVORITE FOOD: Seafood, lobster, steak, spaghetti -- everything!

FAVORITE AUTHOR: Alex Haley

FAVORITE SPORTS HERO: Muhammad Ali

HOBBIES AND INTERESTS: Fixing automobiles and playing Sega Genesis

CHILDREN AND AGES: Daughter, Shay - 4 yrs.

FITNESS AND DIET TIP: Jogging and low calorie intake

LONG-RANGE CAREER GOAL: To own many food franchises

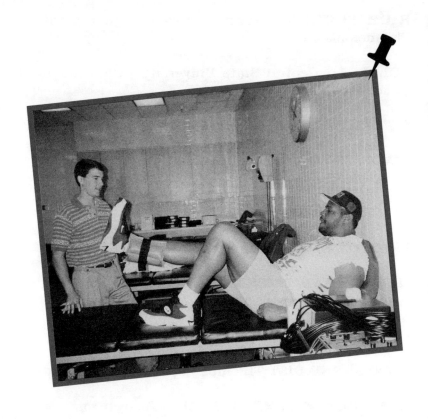

Erik -- working with Jim Maurer, the Cowboys' assistant trainer.

ERIG GEORGE WILLIAMS

ATHLETIC DATA

* Number 79 *
Tackle - 6'6" - 322 lbs.

FIRST PLAYED ORGANIZED FOOTBALL: In the ninth grade at John Bartram High School in Philadelphia

YEARS IN PROFESSIONAL FOOTBALL: 5th year

ENJOY MOST ABOUT BEING WITH THE DALLAS COWBOYS: The winning tradition

HONORS OR AWARDS: Competed in shot put and discus at John Bartram High School; small college All-America as a senior; MVP of the team in 1990; first offensive lineman from Central State University to ever be selected in NFL Draft; Kodak All-America, Sheridan All-America, and NAIA All-America honors; earned first-team All-Pro honors from "Sports Illustrated", and named to All-Madden Team in 1992; in 1993, went to Pro Bowl and was a consensus All-Pro; before an automobile accident on October 24, 1994, was once again proving himself to be one of the top tacklers in the NFL, receiving a game ball for his blocking in Dallas' season opener against Pittsburgh; because of the accident forcing him out of the lineup, it marked the first missed start for Williams in 44 straight games; after the accident, underwent surgery on October 31 to repair his injuries; has become diligent in his rehabilitation and strength workouts, aiming for a healthy return in 1995

TOP: Kevin Williams has the type of athletic ability that makes him a threat to score a touchdown every time he touches the football.

MIDDLE: Kevin's game-breaking ability has been a trademark since he was a high school player at Roosevelt High School in Dallas.

BOTTOM: Williams on a run in preseason game, 1995.

TINA HOWELL & KEVIN WILLIAMS

PERSONAL and ATHLETIC DATA

* Number 85 *
Wide Receiver - 5'9" - 195 lbs.

BORN: Kevin -- 1-25-71

HIGH SCHOOL: Kevin -- Roosevelt High School in Dallas, Texas

COLLEGE: Kevin -- University of Miami (Criminal Justice)

YEARS IN PROFESSIONAL FOOTBALL: 3rd year

HONORS OR AWARDS: Rated as one of nation's top five receivers following senior season in high school; as senior, split time between running back and wide receiver, rushing for 995 yards on 100 carries and 10 touchdowns, while catching 36 passes for 757 yards; career high school statistics are quite remarkable -- 21 receiving touchdowns - 14 rushing touchdowns (17.9 average) - 177 rushing attempts for 1,339 yards (11.4 average) - kickoff return average (25.6) - punt return average (33.2) - averaged 17.1 yards every time touched ball in high school; fastest Hurricane while at Miami with 4.28 speed; as sophomore, drew Heisman Trophy attention -- per attempt averages for season were: receiving (15.7 yards per catch) - rushing (10.8) - punt returns (15.6 - fourth in nation) - and kickoff returns (18.5); returned school-record three punts for touchdowns (one short of NCAA season record); named Kick Returner of the Year by "The Sporting News" in 1991 and Punt Returner of the Year by Football Writers Association of America; Big East Special Teams Player of the Year; elected to enter the NFL after junior season of eligibility; as rookie (1993) touched ball 27 times on offensive plays and scored 4 touchdowns; Cowboys' starting deep man on kickoff and punt returns, was an All-Rookie Team selection as wide receiver by "Football News"; 1994 - became first player in club history to score touchdown on punt return and kickoff return in same season; established new team record for combined kickoff and punt return yardage with 1,497; ranked fourth in NFL in 1994 in kickoff return average with 26.7 yard mark -- third highest single season average in club history; has compiled career averages of 24.8 yards on kickoff returns, 9.7 yards on punt returns, 13.9 yards on pass receptions, 3.5 yards per rushing attempt

TOP: Travis, Kathy, Wade, and Hayden on Thanksgiving, 1994.

BOTTOM: "TRUE BLUE TEXANS" -- Travis and Hayden Wilson.

KATHY & WADE WILSON

PERSONAL DATA

BORN: *Wade* -- 2-1-59 in Greenville, Texas; *Kathy* -- 10-3-59 in Eastland, Texas

HIGH SCHOOL: *Wade* -- Commerce (Texas) High School

COLLEGE: *Wade* -- East Texas State University (Business/ Finance); *Kathy* -- University of Oklahoma (B.S. -- Business Communication/Public Relations)

FAVORITE ACADEMIC SUBJECT: *Wade* -- History; *Kathy* -- Public Relations

FAVORITE TYPE OF MUSIC: *Wade* -- Country and western; *Kathy* -- All kinds

FAVORITE FOOD: *Wade* -- Seafood and Mexican; *Kathy* -- Mexican, pasta, and seafood

FAVORITE AUTHOR: *Kathy* -- John Grisham, Mary Higgins Clark, and Gary Smalley

FAVORITE SPORTS HERO: *Wade* -- Roger Staubach; *Kathy* -- Mike Singletary and Roger Staubach

HOBBIES AND INTERESTS: *Wade* -- Golf, kids, friends, and movies; has SEC-series seven registration and works during off-season as a financial consultant for Merrill-Lynch; devotes much time to American Diabetes Assoc.; *Kathy* -- Photography, her children, reading, movies, friends, and traveling

CHILDREN AND AGES: Travis Wade - 5 yrs.; and Hayden Lee - 2 yrs.

HOW YOU MET SPOUSE: Next door neighbors

FITNESS AND DIET TIP: Exercise consistently, doing things you enjoy; start your day with a good breakfast, and drink plenty of water

LONG-RANGE CAREER GOAL: Have opportunity to work at something I love to do -- just as I have loved playing professional football, and continue to enjoy raising my children

Hayden Lee Wilson with brother, Travis Wade -- 1994.

CHARLES "WADE" WILSON

ATHLETIC DATA

* Number 11 *
Quarterback - 6'3" - 206 lbs.

FIRST PLAYED ORGANIZED FOOTBALL: In seventh grade as quarterback and free safety for Commerce Junior High "Tigers"

YEARS IN PROFESSIONAL FOOTBALL: 15th year (Minnesota Vikings - 11 yrs.; Atlanta Falcons - 1 yr.; New Orleans Saints - 2 yrs.; and 1st year with Dallas)

GREATEST MOMENT IN SPORTS: 12-1-85 -- with Minnesota Vikings, trailing Philadelphia Eagles 23-0 with 8:23 left to play -- threw 3 touchdowns, including 2 to Anthony Carter, in final 4 minutes to lead Vikings to 28-23 victory for greatest comeback in club history

HONORS OR AWARDS: NAIA All-America, as senior at ETSU, led Lone Star Conference in passing and total offense -- named Lone Star Conference's Most Valuable Player; college team MVP - 2 yrs.; All-Madden Team in 1987 -- set eight new club quarterback playoff records, including four season records, three career records, and one single-game record; Pro Bowl, after leading NFC as a quarterback and finishing third overall in the League with a 91.5 quarterback rating-- in 1988; 1989 Mackey Award -- NFC leading passer; 1989 March of Dimes' Viking of the Year; started final three games of 1992 season and passed for over 300 yards in each; had 5 touchdowns at Tampa Bay in 35-7 win over Bucs, marking a career-high and Falcons' single-game record -- overall, in last three games, hit on 80 of 114 for 1,038 yards with 10 touchdowns; tied club record in 1993 when he went three straight games without throwing an interception; stands in top spot on Minnesota Vikings' all-time chart in average gain per attempt; signed with Cowboys on May 22, 1995, as unrestricted free agent from New Orleans; becomes the seventh back-up to Troy Aikman since 1989

TOP: Darren and Juli Woodson with DJ (1-1/2 yrs.)

BOTTOM: Darren, DJ, and Juli at Benihana Restaurant while at Pro Bowl in Hawaii (1995).

JULI & DARREN WOODSON

PERSONAL DATA

BORN: *Darren* -- 4-25-69 in Phoenix, Arizona; *Juli* -- 5-22-70 in Phoenix, Arizona

HIGH SCHOOL: *Darren* -- Maryvale High School in Phoenix

COLLEGE: *Darren* -- Arizona State University (Criminal Justice)

WIFE'S OCCUPATION: Student/homemaker

FAVORITE TYPE OF MUSIC: *Darren* -- Rhythm and blues; *Juli* -- Rhythm and blues, and jazz

FAVORITE FOOD: *Darren* -- "Anything Mom cooks"; *Juli* -- Oriental

FAVORITE AUTHOR: *Juli* -- Judith Krantz

FAVORITE SPORTS HERO: *Darren* -- Walter Payton; *Juli* -- Husband Darren

HOBBIES AND INTERESTS: *Darren* -- Water skiing, basketball, and hanging out with friends and family; *Juli* -- Shopping, snow skiing, and spending time with family in Phoenix

CHILDREN AND AGES: DJ - 3 yrs.

DJ Woodson at home in Dallas.

DARREN RAY WOODSON

ATHLETIC DATA

* Number 28 *
Safety - 6'1" - 215 lbs.

FIRST PLAYED ORGANIZED FOOTBALL: At eight years old as a running back for the "Rebels"

YEARS IN PROFESSIONAL FOOTBALL: 4th year

HONORS OR AWARDS: First-team All-Metro Division AAA linebacker and running back at Maryvale High School in Phoenix; ran a career-high 225 yards and six touchdowns vs. Kofa High in Yuma, Arizona, tying a Phoenix Metro game record and setting a school mark; served as team captain in senior year; earned first-team All-City Honors as linebacker and second-team recognition on offense in final season; honorable mention All-America in 1990 as junior and All-PAC 10 second-team selection as senior; second-round draft choice of Cowboys in 1992; led special teams with 19 tackles in 1992 -- in 16 games recorded 33 tackles (28 solo) -- second among Dallas' rookie tacklers; as second-year player in 1993, earned a starting job at strong safety and nearly won the team's individual tackle title by collecting 155, just shy of team leader -- 155 tackles were the most ever by a Dallas defensive back; with 8 double-digit tackle games in 1993, only second player to register at least 7 double-figure tackle games in a season; led 1993 Cowboys in fumble recoveries with three (while forcing another); team's leading tackler in playoffs with 27 total stops; 1994 was a career-season for Woodson, his second year as a starter; named All-Pro by the Associated Press, "The Sporting News", Pro Football Writers of America, "Football Digest", and "College & Pro Football Newsweekly"; tied for team lead in interceptions, becoming first Dallas defensive back to be selected as a Pro Bowl starter since 1985; tied for third on team in passes defended with 12; earned game balls in six of Cowboys' first seven games in 1994

ROOKIES

TOP: Eric Bjornson -- a backup to Pro Bowler Jay Novacek, with similar potential as an offensive threat.

BOTTOM: Bjornson, a fourth-round draft choice, was taken with the highest pick ever used by Dallas on a University of Washington player.

ERIC BJORNSON

PERSONAL and ATHLETIC DATA

* Number 86 *
Tight End - 6'4" - 230 lbs.

BORN: 12-15-71 in San Francisco, California

HIGH SCHOOL: Bishop O'Dowd High School in Oakland

COLLEGE: University of Washington (Sociology)

YEARS IN PROFESSIONAL FOOTBALL: Rookie

FIRST PLAYED ORGANIZED FOOTBALL: As quarterback for the "Dragons"

GREATEST MOMENT IN SPORTS: Beating Miami in the Orange Bowl to end their home winning streak

FAVORITE TYPE OF MUSIC: Classic rock

FAVORITE FOOD: Pasta

FAVORITE AUTHOR: Dean Koontz

FAVORITE SPORTS HERO: Joe Montana

HOBBIES: Movies and baseball

HONORS OR AWARDS: Starred at Bishop O'Dowd High School as a three-year starter at quarterback, while earning scholar-athlete awards from the "Oakland Tribune" and the National Football Foundation Hall of Fame with his 4.02 GPA; 2nd team All-PAC 10 and Academic All-America honors; was sixth in the PAC-10 in receptions and tied for second in touchdown catches; Washington Male Athlete of the Year; Dallas Cowboys' fourth-round draft choice in 1995

TOP: Alundis Brice, having just completed his senior season at Ole Miss, tried to play the role of peacemaker during an on-campus altercation, and was shot in the chest, with the bullet nearly hitting his heart -- 11 days in the hospital, including two days in critical condition.

BOTTOM: Though the 1995 Draft became very uncertain, his physical rehabilitation progressed at a dramatic rate, and the Cowboys used a fourth-round selection on Brice.

ALUNDIS BRICE

PERSONAL and ATHLETIC DATA

* Number 29 *
Cornerback - 5'10" - 178 lbs.

BORN: 5-1-70 in Brookhaven, Mississippi

HIGH SCHOOL: Brookhaven High School

COLLEGE: University of Mississippi (Social Work)

YEARS IN PROFESSIONAL FOOTBALL: Rookie

HONORS OR AWARDS: First-team, Class 5A, All-State selection as a senior in high school; three-year letterman in track -- winning state title in the 200 meters; standout member of the Ole Miss track team, registered personal best times of 10.75 (100 meters), 21.62 (200 meters), and 6.22 (55 meters); as junior All-SEC selection at cornerback in 1993, returned two of his seven interceptions on the year for touchdowns -- becoming only the second player in school history to accomplish that feat in one season; seven thefts were returned for an average of 14.0 yards per effort and his touchdowns were scored on interception returns of 45 yards and 46 yards; as a senior in 1994, was a first-team All Southeastern Conference and a second-team All-America selection; third player in Ole Miss history to record at least seven interceptions in one season; selected as the Chuckie Mullins Courage Award winner; as Rebels' left cornerback in 1994, contributed 50 tackles (42 solos) and 9 passes defensed, registering three interceptions in the first five games of the year; Dallas Cowboys' fourth-round draft choice in 1995

Billy Davis -- wide receiver from the University of Pittsburgh.

BILLY DAVIS

PERSONAL and ATHLETIC DATA

* Number 87 *
Safety/Wide Receiver - 6'1" - 199 lbs.

BORN: 7-6-72 in Texas

HIGH SCHOOL: Irvin High School in El Paso, Texas

COLLEGE: University of Pittsburgh

YEARS IN PROFESSIONAL FOOTBALL: Rookie

HONORS OR AWARDS: Earned All-District, All-City, and All-Region honors in football as a quarterback, and All-District and All-City honors in track as a senior in high school; after making 11 catches for 100 yards as a freshman, Davis tallied 34 catches for 503 yards (14.8) and three touchdowns in twelve games as a sophomore at Pittsburgh; as a junior, started nine of eleven games and made 24 receptions for 346 yards (14.4) with one touchdown; started 10 of the 11 games he played in as a senior and recorded 51 receptions for 731 yards (14.3 average) and nine touchdowns; finished career at Pitt in third place on the Panthers' all-time receptions list with 120 and in fifth place on Pitt's all-time receiving yardage chart with 1,680

Fieldings (Number 54) backs up at middle and strongside linebacker.

ANTHONY FIELDINGS

PERSONAL and ATHLETIC DATA

* Number 54 *
Linebacker - 6"1" - 237 lbs.

BORN: 7-9-71, in Florida

COLLEGE: Morningside College (Psychology and Criminal Justice)

FAVORITE SUBJECT: Social studies and science

YEARS IN PROFESSIONAL FOOTBALL: 1st year

HONORS OR AWARDS: Set Morningside College record for tackles in a season (151 in 1991); was Defensive Player of the Game nine times in his collegiate career; played on 1992 defense that yielded only 104 rushing yards per game; was 1992 preseason All-America pick by Street and Smith; went to training camp with Buffalo in 1993 and 1994; led Rhein Fire in World League with 95 tackles last season and was defensive MVP; signed with Dallas on July 31, 1995

HOBBIES AND INTERESTS: Likes to draw and play chess

CHILDREN AND AGES: Anthony - 2 yrs.

LONG-RANGE CAREER GOAL: To set up a youth shelter for at-risk kids in Orlando, central Florida area, or maybe even in Miami

Edward Hervey -- a rare combination of size and speed in a wide receiver.

EDWARD HERVEY

PERSONAL and ATHLETIC DATA

* Number 81 *
Wide Receiver - 6'3" - 179 lbs.

BORN: 5-4-73 in Houston, Texas

HIGH SCHOOL: Compton (California) High School

COLLEGE: University of Southern California (History)

YEARS IN PROFESSIONAL FOOTBALL: Rookie

HONORS OR AWARDS: Starred as quarterback and wide receiver in high school; member of the All-Moore League team in football following senior year; ran leg on school's California state champion 400-meter relay squad; as quarterback at Pasadena City College, earned Cal-Hi Sports Junior College All-State and All-Mission Conference honors in 1992, averaging 171 yards of total offense, passing for 919 yards and three touchdowns on 78-of-143 passes, and running for 791 yards and eight touchdowns on 169 carries; three-time Mission Conference Player of the Week and MVP of Rose City Classic Bowl; as freshman, rushed for 137 yards on 26 carries and completed 12-of-28 passes for 116 yards and one touchdown; transferred to Southern Cal in fall of 1993, where he was a standout quarterback; first year as wide receiver for Trojans, saw action in 11 of 13 games, starting three of the first six games; following spring football, joined Trojan track team and qualified for the finals in the 200 meters at the PAC-10 Championships; earned All-America honors in three events at the NCAA Track and Field Championships in spring of senior year; fifth-round draft choice of the Dallas Cowboys in 1995

TOP: Oscar Sturgis -- a quick, aggressive pass rusher who knows how to use his size and leaping ability to bat down passes at the line of scrimmage.

BOTTOM: Sturgis adds depth to the defensive line of the NFL's top-ranked defense.

OSCAR STURGIS

PERSONAL and ATHLETIC DATA

* Number 90 *
Defensive End - 6'5" - 280 lbs.

BORN: 1-12-71 in Hamlet, North Carolina

HIGH SCHOOL: Fork Union Military Academy in 1990; previously, Richmond County (North Carolina) High School

COLLEGE: University of North Carolina - Chapel Hill (Sociology)

GREATEST MOMENT IN SPORTS: When he scored two touchdowns on defense in senior year

YEARS IN PROFESSIONAL FOOTBALL: Rookie

HONORS OR AWARDS: Super Prep All-America selection; Associated Press and "Greensboro News & Record" All-State selection as tight end; led team to a pair of state titles in 1988-1989, accumulating perfect 30-0 record; as senior, caught 32 passes for 776 yards and 11 touchdowns; ACC Player of the Week, twice in row, as senior at North Carolina; selected to Senior Bowl and East-West Shrine Game in senior year; last two seasons, credited with 18 quarterback pressures while batting down 10 passes; drafted by Dallas Cowboys in the 7th round in 1995

FAVORITE TYPE OF MUSIC: Rhythm and blues, slow, hip hop, and jazz

FAVORITE FOOD: Mom's fried chicken

FAVORITE AUTHOR: Maya Angelou and her book of poems

FAVORITE SPORTS HERO: "My father, because he allowed me to play sports"

HOBBIES AND INTERESTS: Reading, listening to music, hang out, and playing Sega

PETS: Dog - "Seiko"

Kendell Watkins -- the only 300-pound tight end in the NFL.

KENDELL MAIRO WATKINS

PERSONAL and ATHLETIC DATA

* Number 83 *
Tight End - 6'1" - 305 lbs.

BORN: 3-8-73 in Jackson, Mississippi

HIGH SCHOOL: Provine High School in Jackson

COLLEGE: Mississippi State University (Political Science)

FAVORITE ACADEMIC SUBJECT: English

GREATEST MOMENT IN SPORTS: Being drafted by the Dallas Cowboys when people doubted it

YEARS IN PROFESSIONAL FOOTBALL: Rookie

FIRST PLAYED ORGANIZED FOOTBALL: In ninth grade as a tight end/linebacker for the Hardy Junior High "Rebels"

HONORS OR AWARDS: Earned All-Metro, All-District, and second-team All-State honors as a tight end in high school; team captain his senior year; as a senior at Mississippi State, accounted for 5 receptions, 66 yards receiving, and 44 knockdown blocks; an All-Southeast Conference selection as a senior, is one of the best blocking tight ends to enter the NFL in years; second-round draft choice by Dallas Cowboys in 1995

FAVORITE TYPE OF MUSIC: Rap

FAVORITE FOOD: Pasta and meat sauce

FAVORITE AUTHOR: Langston Hughes

FAVORITE SPORTS HERO: Shaq

HOBBIES AND INTERESTS: Music, relaxing, and playing with my daughter

CHILDREN AND AGES: Breana Pendleton - 1 yr.

Charlie Williams is a versatile player who lined up at receiver, safety, and special teams at Bowling Green State University.

CHARLIE WILLIAMS

PERSONAL and ATHLETIC DATA

* Number 42 *
Safety - 6'0" - 190 lbs.

BORN: 2-2-72 in Michigan

HIGH SCHOOL: Henry Ford High School in Detroit

COLLEGE: Bowling Green State University (Sociology)

YEARS IN PROFESSIONAL FOOTBALL: Rookie

HONORS OR AWARDS: All-City and All-Public Schools League selection as a junior and senior in high school; made 25 career touchdown catches and 12 career interceptions in high school; in one game as a junior, caught eight passes, scored three touchdowns, and intercepted two passes; the special teams captain at Bowling Green as a senior, contributed five catches for 62 yards on offense, 31 tackles, two defensed passes and an interception on defense, and blocked a kick on special teams; a special teams standout with superb leaping ability, blocked six kicks during his collegiate career; with 40-yard dash speed of 4.41, has the quickness to stay deep with receivers and is a punishing tackler; first player ever drafted from Bowling Green State University by the Dallas Cowboys; drafted in third round, Williams will be looking to join the ranks of Erik Wiliams and Leon Lett as players from small schools who have become major contributors for the Cowboys; led team in special teams tackles in 1995 preseason with four

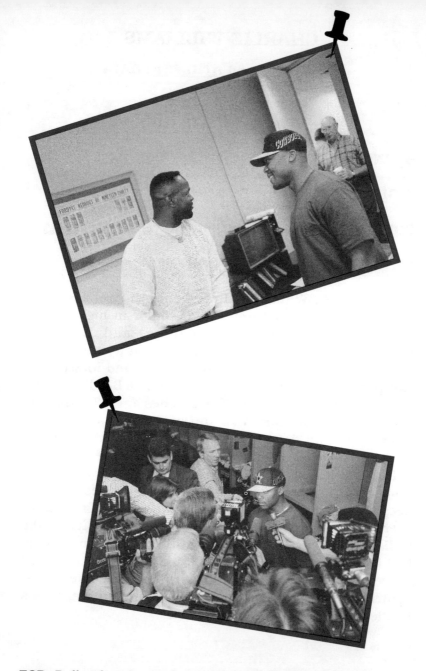

TOP: Dallas found a backup to Emmitt Smith in their second-round selection of Sherman Williams from Alabama.

BOTTOM: Williams is a compact back who has powerful legs, great field instincts, and catches the ball well.

SHERMAN WILLIAMS

PERSONAL and ATHLETIC DATA

* Number 20 *
Running Back - 5'8" - 190 lbs.

BORN: 8-13-73 in Alabama

HIGH SCHOOL: Blount High School in Mobile, Alabama

COLLEGE: University of Alabama (Sports Fitness Management)

YEARS IN PROFESSIONAL FOOTBALL: Rookie

HONORS OR AWARDS: Named All-State by the Alabama Sportswriters Association as a senior, when he led Blount High School to Class 5A state title; during senior season, rushed for 3,004 yards and 31 touchdowns, becoming first player in Alabama prep history to rush for over 3,000 yards in a season; played in eight games as freshman at Alabama in 1991, rushing for 108 yards and two touchdowns in 12 attempts; as sophomore, played in every game as a backup running back, and tallied 299 yards on 64 rushes, scoring eight touchdowns; 1993, as a junior, took over the starting running back job in third game of season and opened year with five straight 100-yard games, including 148 yards on 24 carries against Arkansas -- finished season with 738 rushing yards on 168 carries with nine touchdowns; a finalist for Doak Walker Award, finished Alabama career with 1,341 yards rushing, second-best season total in school history; his 291 carries broke the Tide's season record of 238; finished season averaging 138.5 all-purpose yards per game, the sixteenth best in the nation; recorded seven 100-yard rushing days and two 99-yard efforts for senior year; Dallas' first draft choice in 1995, second-round selection; led team in rushing in three of the five 1995 preseason games

#40 - Bill Bates   **#84** - Jay Novacek
#22 - Emmitt Smith and **#88** - Michael Irvin
#88 - Michael Irvin   **#78** - Leon Lett

COACHING
STAFF

TOP: Axe and Gloria Alexander at home.

BOTTOM: Gloria and Axe leaving for the evening.

GLORIA & HUBBARD L. ALEXANDER

PERSONAL DATA

BORN: Hubbard Lindsey "Axe" -- 2-14-39 (Winston-Salem, North Carolina); Gloria -- 9-9-

HIGH SCHOOL: Axe -- Atkins High School in Winston-Salem, North Carolina

COLLEGE: Axe -- Tennessee State University (B.S. -- Health and Physical Education); Gloria -- Tennessee State University (B.S. -- Education); University of Memphis (M.Ed.)

WIFE'S OCCUPATION: Second grade teacher at Sheffield Primary in Carrollton, Farmers Branch

FAVORITE TYPE OF MUSIC: Axe -- Jazz; Gloria -- Blues

FAVORITE FOOD: Axe -- Blackened/Cajun seafood; Gloria -- Seafood

FAVORITE AUTHOR: Axe -- James Baldwin; Gloria -- Terry McMillan

FAVORITE SPORTS HERO: Gloria -- Michael Jordan

HOBBIES AND INTERESTS: Axe -- Computer solitaire, power walking, and listening to music; Gloria -- Decorating home, collecting Afro-American art and collectibles (especially Christmas items); and teaching children

CHILDREN AND AGES: Todd - 29 yrs.; Chad - 20 yrs.; and Bard - 15 yrs.

PETS: "Simba" - 8-month-old Cocker Spaniel

FITNESS AND DIET TIP: Count calories, eat low fat diet, and walk daily

TOP: Alexanders' sons: (left to right) Todd, Bard, and Chad

BOTTOM: Chad, junior at Wake Forest University; and Bard, sophomore at Coppell High.

HUBBARD LINDSEY ALEXANDER

PROFESSIONAL DATA

ASSISTANT COACH
Wide Receivers

YEARS IN PROFESSIONAL FOOTBALL: 6th season with the Dallas Cowboys

ENJOY MOST ABOUT BEING WITH THE DALLAS COWBOYS: "There is nothing about my job that I don't enjoy"

EXPERIENCE, HONORS, AND AWARDS: Earned All-America honors as three-year starter at center at Tennessee State -- signed as a free agent with Dallas; began coaching career with alma mater in 1962; after seven seasons as a very successful high school coach in Memphis, spent six seasons as an assistant at Vanderbilt University; coached ten seasons at University of Miami, developing three of the school's all-time leading receivers in 1987; three of his Miami receivers have recently led their respective NFL clubs in receiving; his receiving unit blossomed into one of the NFL's finest in 1992 -- Dallas' starting receivers combination of Irvin and Harper accounted for 11.3 catches for 1,958 yards; in 1993, Irving was named as the starting wide receiver in his third consecutive Pro Bowl, finished as NFL's second-ranked receiver in yardage, and was the third-ranked receiver in catches; Harper surpassed his career highs in receptions and finished second in NFL in yards per catch; in 1994, Alexander's wide receiving corps helped lead Cowboys' offense to an average gain-per-pass play of 12.3 yards, the second highest average in the NFL; Irvin earned his fourth consecutive Pro Bowl appearance, ending season with five 100-yard receiving games, adding two more during the play-offs; his 12 catch, 192-yard performance against San Francisco in NFC Championship Game tied a career high for receptions and set a new career mark for receiving yards; Kevin Williams, used mostly on third down passing situations, flourished down the stretch, catching six passes for 107 yards, a 17.8 average, in five of the last eight games; Williams tallied six catches for 78 yards in the NFC Championship game against San Francisco

TOP: Jane and Neill Armstrong.

BOTTOM: Armstrong family: David and family; Neill, Jr., and family; and Gail Farden and family.

JANE & NEILL ARMSTRONG

PERSONAL and PROFESSIONAL DATA

BORN: Neill -- 3-9-26 in Tishomingo, Oklahoma; Jane -- 4-11-25 in Neosho, Missouri

COLLEGE: Neill -- Oklahoma State University (B.S.); Jane -- Oklahoma State University

FIRST PLAYED ORGANIZED FOOTBALL: In high school for the Tishomingo "Indians"

YEARS IN PROFESSIONAL FOOTBALL: 33 years in professional football; with the Cowboys since 1982

ENJOY MOST ABOUT BEING WITH THE DALLAS COWBOYS: The association with all of the people in the organization

EXPERIENCE, HONORS, AND AWARDS: Football All-America honors; played with Philadelphia Eagles (1947-1951); Canadian Football (1952-1954); coached Oklahoma State University (1955-1961) and Houston Oilers (1962-1963); Head Coach in Edmonton Canada (1964-1969); coached Minnesota Vikings (1969-1977); Head Coach of Chicago Bears (1978-1981)

FAVORITE TYPE OF MUSIC: Neill -- Country/western, semi-classical, and big band; Jane -- Big band and semi-classical

FAVORITE FOOD: Neill -- Black-eyed peas, cornbread, and chicken-fried steak; Jane -- Grilled chicken

FAVORITE AUTHOR: Neill -- John Grisham; Jane -- Mary Higgins Clark

FAVORITE SPORTS HERO: Neill -- Sammy Baugh (retired); Jane -- Nolan Ryan

HOBBIES AND INTERESTS: Neill -- Golf and fishing; Jane -- Bridge, volunteering, and football

CHILDREN AND AGES: Neill, Jr. - 48 yrs.; David - 44 yrs.; Gail - 40 yrs.; and five grandchildren

TOP: Tony – signing letter of intent to play basketball at Angelo State University. *(from left)* Coach Mike Ray, Tony, Joe, and Diann.

BOTTOM: *(from left)* Con Hunley, Collin Raye, Diann and Joe, and Scotty Raye – at Troy Aikman's gala for his golf tournament.

DIANN & JOE AVEZZANO

PERSONAL DATA

BORN: *Joe* -- 11-17-43 in Yonkers, New York; *Diann* -- 3-10-49 in Story City, Iowa

HIGH SCHOOL: *Joe* -- Jackson High School in Miami, Florida

COLLEGE: *Joe* -- Florida State University (Criminology); *Diann* -- Patricia Stevens (Fashion Merchandising)

WIFE'S OCCUPATION: Runs own small business of wholesale costume jewelry

FAVORITE TYPE OF MUSIC: *Joe* -- Like all kinds -- mainly rhythm and blues, and country; *Diann* -- All music

FAVORITE FOOD: *Joe* -- Italian; *Diann* -- Sushi

FAVORITE SPORTS HERO: *Diann* -- Hank Aaron

HOBBIES AND INTERESTS: *Joe* -- Music and weight training; *Diann* -- Music and lifting weights

HONORS OR AWARDS: *Joe* -- President of student body; raised over $80,000 for Special Olympics through yearly Special Olympics Concert at "Cowboy's Country and Western Club"; *Diann* -- Female lead in high school musical all four years; sang professionally while living in Pittsburgh

CHILDREN AND AGES: Tony - 19 yrs.

PETS: Cat - "Butterscotch"

FITNESS AND DIET TIP: Eat most anything you want, but just eat a moderate amount; use it -- or lose it!

TOP: *(left to right)* Diann and Joe with Brill Garrett and Pono Tuinei -- at Texfest, 1995.

BOTTOM: Tony *(far right)* with two teammates from Maine Central Institute prep school.

JOSEPH (JOE) W. AVEZZANO

PROFESSIONAL DATA

ASSISTANT COACH
Special Teams

FIRST PLAYED ORGANIZED FOOTBALL: In the ninth grade for the Boys Club

YEARS IN PROFESSIONAL FOOTBALL: 5th season with the Dallas Cowboys

ENJOY MOST ABOUT BEING WITH THE DALLAS COWBOYS: Enjoying a good positive working environment for my family in a great city

EXPERIENCE, HONORS, AND AWARDS: Played at Jackson High School under current Cowboys' Coach Joe Brodsky; starred at guard for Florida State -- drafted by Boston Patriots; began coaching career at Washington High School in Massillon, Ohio, in 1967; coached at Florida State before joining Iowa State in 1969; offensive line coach at Pittsburgh (1973-1976), helping '76 Panthers to a national title; from 1977-1979, served as offensive coordinator at Tennessee; spent five seasons as head coach at Oregon State from 1977-1979; coached offensive line at Texas A & M for four seasons, during which time Aggies won three Southwest Conference titles and two Cotton Bowls -- took on duties of offensive coordinator in 1988; named NFL Special Teams Coach of the Year, in 1991, by widest margin ever; in 1992, Dallas special teams led entire NFL in team-punt-return average; under Joe's guidance, Dallas was recognized as perhaps NFL's most productive team in the kicking game for second straight year; named NFL's Special Team Coach in 1993 -- for second time in three years; in Super Bowl season of 1993, Cowboys were only team in NFL to finish regular season with a Top 10 ranking in all four major kicking game categories; in addition to building very productive coverage and return units, Cowboys have established a well-deserved reputation for making the big play; since joining the Dallas Cowboys, Avezzano's units have been responsible for 11 blocked kicks; in last three seasons, Kevin Williams and Kelvin Martin combined to return five punts for touchdowns

Robert and Diana Blackwell in Creede, Colorado - June, 1995.

DIANA & ROBERT BLACKWELL

PERSONAL DATA

BORN: *Robert* -- 12-1-50 in Dallas, Texas; *Diana* -- 5-25-58 in Louisville, Kentucky

HIGH SCHOOL: *Robert* -- Garland High School (suburb of Dallas, Texas)

COLLEGE: *Robert* -- Stephen F. Austin State University (B.S. -- Communications); *Diana* -- Moorpark Junior College (A.A.) and California Lutheran College

WIFE'S OCCUPATION: Flight attendant for American Airlines

HONORS OR AWARDS: *Robert* -- Became a member of the SAR (Sons of the American Revolution); *Diana* -- 1993 Professional Flight Attendant Award; and two years Perfect Attendance Award at American Airlines

FAVORITE TYPE OF MUSIC: *Robert* -- Classic rock and country; *Diana* -- Pop rock and classic rock

FAVORITE FOOD: *Robert* -- Mexican; *Diana* -- Seafood

FAVORITE AUTHOR: *Robert* -- Mark Twain; *Diana* -- John Grisham

FAVORITE SPORTS HERO: *Robert* -- Mickey Mantle; *Diana* -- Michael Jordan

HOBBIES AND INTERESTS: *Robert* -- Fly fishing, golf, his family, and coaching son's soccer and baseball teams; *Diana* -- Coppell Women's Club, Mom's in Touch, decorating, crafts, reading, family, and PTO -- assistant field day coordinator

CHILDREN AND AGES: Nathaniel Rivers - 8 yrs.; Lora Ann - 14 months

PETS: Sheltie -- four-year-old "Lady"

TOP: Robert and Diana -- at American Bowl in Toronto, Canada (8-12-95).

BOTTOM: Diana (holding Lora), Nate, and Robert -- at Coppell Kids Country in August, 1995.

ROBERT GLENN BLACKWELL

PROFESSIONAL DATA

Video Director

YEARS IN PROFESSIONAL FOOTBALL: 15 years

ENJOY MOST ABOUT BEING WITH THE DALLAS COWBOYS: The feeling that everyone in the organization is working towards one goal (WINNING!) . . . and being able to see the results of your work on a weekly basis

EXPERIENCE, HONORS, AND AWARDS: Enters seventh season as the Dallas Cowboys' Video Director, after eight seasons as an assistant with Dallas; in charge of taping and editing all Cowboys' practices and games; edits opponents' tapes; handles all of the team's photographic needs; shot coaching game films for basketball and football at Southern Methodist University from 1979-1984; after earning degree from Stephen F. Austin University, produced a film on the efforts to save the red wolf from extinction for the U. S. Fish and Wildlife Service; the following year, served as director of photography on a film about the North Atlantic Indian migrations for Gulf Oil and the State of Texas

Freda and John Blake -- celebrating their wedding anniversary.

FREDA & JOHN BLAKE

PERSONAL DATA

BORN: *John* -- 3-6-61 in Rockford, Illinois; *Freda* -- 4-15-62 in Tulsa, Oklahoma

HIGH SCHOOL: *John* -- Charles Page High School in Sand Springs, Oklahoma

COLLEGE: *John* -- University of Oklahoma (B.S. -- Public Relations and Recreation); *Freda* -- Central State University (B.B.A. -- Business Management; Minor in Marketing)

WIFE'S OCCUPATION: Financial analyst

FAVORITE TYPE OF MUSIC: *John* and *Freda* -- Jazz

FAVORITE FOOD: *John* -- Baked fish and non-fat vanilla yogurt; *Freda* -- Pasta dishes and salads

FAVORITE AUTHOR: *John* -- Alex Haley; *Freda* -- Alice Walker

FAVORITE SPORTS HERO: *John* -- Leroy Selmon; *Freda* -- Michael Jordan

HOBBIES AND INTERESTS: *John* -- Fishing and hunting; *Freda* -- Interior decorating

FITNESS AND DIET TIP: For a healthy mind and body, forty-five minute work out -- at least three times a week; drink an 8-oz. glass of water eight times a day; and maintain low-fat meals

John and Freda on an Alaskan cruise in summer, 1995.

JOHN BLAKE

PROFESSIONAL DATA

ASSISTANT COACH
Defensive Line

FIRST PLAYED ORGANIZED FOOTBALL: In 1974, as fullback and nose guard for the Clyde Boyd Junior High "Trojans"

YEARS IN PROFESSIONAL FOOTBALL: 3rd season with the Dallas Cowboys

ENJOY MOST ABOUT BEING WITH THE DALLAS COWBOYS: The overall commitment to success, and the winning attitude of everyone that's a part of the Cowboys' organization

EXPERIENCE, HONORS, AND AWARDS: Highly-recruited All-State pick at Charles Page High School in Sand Springs, Oklahoma; played nose tackle at Oklahoma from 1980-1983; earned All-Big Eight Conference Defense Lineman; was a big part of building a top-rated defense while coaching at Oklahoma from 1989-1992; in 1988, named one of the Outstanding Young Men in America; in first year as the Cowboys' defensive line coach, helped guide defensive tackle Russell Maryland to the Pro Bowl, the first such honor for a Dallas defensive lineman since Randy White was selected in 1985; under Blake, the Dallas' defense proved to be one of the league's stingiest, allowing a club record low 21 touchdowns -- good for second in the NFL; in second year as the Cowboys' defensive line coach, the Cowboys became the NFL's top-ranked defense for the second time in three seasons -- among those that contributed to the defensive line's resurgence were defensive end Charles Haley and defensive tackle Leon Lett, who both landed in the Pro Bowl following the season -- the first time since 1983 that the Dallas Cowboys have sent two defensive linemen

TOP: Craig Boller with close friend, Jane Robenstein.

BOTTOM: (from left) Daughters, Valerie and Kimberly, with Craig.

CRAIG BOLLER

PERSONAL and PROFESSIONAL DATA

BORN: 1-29-48 in Belmond, Iowa

COLLEGE: Iowa State University -- Ames (B.S.)

FAVORITE ACADEMIC SUBJECT: Algebra

FIRST PLAYED ORGANIZED FOOTBALL: As a fullback/ linebacker in junior high school in Belmond

YEARS IN PROFESSIONAL FOOTBALL: 1st season with the Dallas Cowboys

GREATEST MOMENT IN SPORTS: Upsetting nationally-ranked Nebraska in 1993 while an assistant coach at Iowa State

EXPERIENCE IN COACHING: 1971-1973 -- Knoxville High School (Knoxville, Iowa); 1974-1976 -- William Penn College (Oskaloosa, Iowa); 1977 -- University of Tennessee (Knoxville, Tennessee); 1978-1979 -- Memphis State University (Memphis, Tennessee); 1980-1986 -- Oregon State University (Corvallis, Oregon); 1987-1994 -- Iowa State University (Ames, Iowa)

FAVORITE TYPE OF MUSIC: Oldies and big bands

FAVORITE SPORTS HERO: Harmon Killebrew

HOBBIES AND INTERESTS: Boating, fishing, golf, and interior decorating

CHILDREN AND AGES: Daughters: Valerie - 28 yrs.; and Kimberly - 24 yrs.

PET PEEVE: Poor listeners

FITNESS AND DIET TIP: Avoid being uncomfortable when eating, and get plenty of rest

LONG-RANGE CAREER GOAL: Coaching in NFL

The Brodsky Family.

JOYCE & JOE BRODSKY

PERSONAL DATA

BORN: *Joe* -- 6-9-34 in Miami, Florida; *Joyce* -- in Brooklyn, New York

HIGH SCHOOL: *Joe* -- Jackson High School in Miami

COLLEGE: Joe -- University of Florida (B.S. and M.S. -- Administration and Supervision); *Joyce* -- University of Miami (B.A. -- Education)

WIFE'S OCCUPATION: Retired English teacher and travel agent

FAVORITE TYPE OF MUSIC: *Joe* -- Country/western and classical; *Joyce* -- Pop, country, and classical

FAVORITE FOOD: Joe -- Lobster and stone crabs; *Joyce* -- Rack of lamb and rice pilaf

FAVORITE AUTHOR: *Joyce* -- James Michener, Leon Uris, and Ken Follet

FAVORITE SPORTS HERO: *Joe* -- His high school basketball coach, Joe McNulty; *Joyce* -- Larry Brodsky

HOBBIES AND INTERESTS: *Joe* -- Golf, fishing, and family; *Joyce* -- Taking care of grandchildren (Amanda - 7 yrs.; and Joey - 4 yrs.); reading, all sports, singing, and traveling

HONORS OR AWARDS: *Joyce* -- Graduated cum laude from the University of Miami, and valedictorian of senior class

CHILDREN AND AGES: Joe, Jr. - 37 yrs. (wife: Robin; and two grandchildren: Amanda and Joey); Larry - 34 yrs.; Jeffrey - 32 yrs. (wife: Frances)

FITNESS AND DIET TIP: Walk, at least 50 minutes, 3 times a week -- about 3 miles each time; eat no red meats or fried foods; eat lots of fruits and vegetables

LONG-RANGE CAREER GOAL: Win Super Bowl XXX -- need a third ring for third son!

Joyce and Joe Brodsky.

JOSEPH (JOE) BRODSKY

PROFESSIONAL DATA

ASSISTANT COACH
Running Backs

YEARS IN PROFESSIONAL FOOTBALL: 7th season with the Dallas Cowboys

ENJOY MOST ABOUT BEING WITH THE DALLAS COWBOYS: Camaraderie of the coaches and quality of the players as people

EXPERIENCE, HONORS, AND AWARDS: Four-year letterman in football, basketball, and track at University of Florida; for thirteen seasons, one of South Florida's most successful high school coaches; won State Football Championship while coaching high school; had first team in the state to go 14-0; while coaching running backs at University of Miami for eleven seasons, won two National Championships; in 1992, helped guide his prized pupil (third-year running back Emmitt Smith) to his second straight NFL rushing title, becoming the first NFL player to lead the League in consecutive years since 1983-1984; Smith became the first running back in League history to record four consecutive seasons with over 1,400 yards rushing, when he topped the mark in 1994; Daryl Johnston earned a second trip to Hawaii for the Pro Bowl in 1994, the only fullback chosen in the NFC for two straight years; Brodsky has been a key ingredient in the Cowboys' struggle from the bottom of the NFL heap to a spot at the top . . . with 1994 as no exception!

TOP: Amy and Bucky Buchanan -- having dinner at the Pro Bowl.

BOTTOM: Bucky -- sightseeing in Hawaii while at Pro Bowl.

AMY & BUCKY BUCHANAN

PERSONAL DATA

BORN: *William Andrew (Bucky)* -- 6-9-61 in Alexandria, Virginia; Amy -- 4-3-65 in Little Rock, Arkansas

HIGH SCHOOL: *Bucky* -- Plano High School in Plano, Texas

WIFE'S OCCUPATION: Administrative Assistant at EDS

FAVORITE TYPE OF MUSIC: *Bucky* -- Rock 'n roll; Amy -- All kinds

FAVORITE FOOD: *Bucky* -- Steak and potatoes

HOBBIES AND INTERESTS: *Bucky* -- Golf, sports of all kinds, and family; Amy -- Water skiing, football, and family

HOW MET: Met through mutual friends -- celebrated tenth-year wedding anniversary in May, 1995

CHILDREN AND AGES: William (Thomas), II - 9 yrs.; and Jonathan (Brett) - 6 yrs.

PETS: Cocker Spaniel, adopted last year - "Barney"

TOP: Brett's school picture in May, 1995.

BOTTOM: Thomas -- ready to play (October, 1994).

WILLIAM A. (BUCKY) BUCHANAN

PROFESSIONAL DATA

Assistant Equipment Manager

YEARS IN PROFESSIONAL FOOTBALL: 2nd season with the Dallas Cowboys

ENJOY MOST ABOUT BEING WITH THE DALLAS COWBOYS: The people treat you like part of a family

EXPERIENCE: Entering second year as the assistant equipment manager of the Dallas Cowboys; though officially joined the Cowboys in 1994, spent many weekends and summers in the equipment room helping his father, "Buck" Buchanan, the Cowboys equipment manager from 1973-1993; before coming to the Dallas Cowboys, spent 1-1/2 years with Willis Medical in Richardson, Texas, and ten years with the Skaggs Alpha Beta grocery store chain

Kay and Dave Campo.

KAY & DAVE CAMPO

PERSONAL DATA

BORN: *Dave* -- 7-18-47 in New London, Connecticut; *Kay* -- 7-22-56 in Ogden, Utah

HIGH SCHOOL: *Dave* -- Robert E. Fitch High School in Groton, Connecticut

COLLEGE: *Dave* -- Central Connecticut State University (B.S. -- Physical Education); Albany State University (M.S. -- Education Communications); *Kay* -- Stevens Henager College

FAVORITE TYPE OF MUSIC: *Dave* -- 50's rock and roll and musical sound tracks; *Kay* -- Country and easy listening

FAVORITE FOOD: *Dave* -- Italian; *Kay* -- Chinese

FAVORITE AUTHOR: *Dave* -- Tom Clancy; *Kay* -- John Grisham

FAVORITE SPORTS HERO: *Dave* -- Frank Gifford

HOBBIES AND INTERESTS: *Dave* -- Music, sports, and golf; *Kay* -- Crafts, reading, and her children

CHILDREN AND AGES: Angie - 21 yrs.; Eric - 19 yrs.; Becky - 18 yrs.; Tommy - 16 yrs.; Shelbie - 15 yrs.; and Michael - 4 yrs.

FITNESS AND DIET TIP: Stay active, eat low-fat diet, and drink lots of water

Campo children: *(back)* Angie and Shelbie; *(front)* Eric and Michael.

DAVID CROSS (DAVE) CAMPO

PROFESSIONAL DATA

ASSISTANT COACH
Defensive Coordinator

FIRST PLAYED ORGANIZED FOOTBALL: As a running back and defensive back for Robert E. Fitch, Sr., High School "Falcons" in Groton, Connecticut

YEARS IN PROFESSIONAL FOOTBALL: 6th season with the Dallas Cowboys

ENJOY MOST ABOUT BEING WITH THE DALLAS COWBOYS: Enjoy being in an organization with great tradition and a commitment to winning, and working in a game I love for twelve months a year at the top level of competition

EXPERIENCE, HONORS, AND AWARDS: Starring at defensive back in college, twice earned All-East honors at shortstop at Central Connecticut State; received Alumni Distinguished Service Award from Central Connecticut State University in 1991; in 1992, Man of the Year from the Southeastern Connecticut Amateur Athletic Association; in 1993, while directing the secondary of the Super Bowl XXVIII Champion Cowboys, Campo's group was led by cornerback Kevin Smith, who intercepted more passes than any other Dallas player since the 1986 season; also in 1993, strong safety Thomas Everett became the first Dallas defensive back to be selected to appear in the Pro Bowl in seven seasons; in 1994, helped direct Dallas defense to the Number One overall defensive ranking in the NFL; under Campo's direction, the Dallas secondary has grown into one of the team's deepest and most productive units over the past five years; elevated to the position of Defensive Coordinator for the Dallas Cowboys in January, 1995

TOP: Rich and Ros, with Kim and Clay -- enjoying New Smyrna Beach, Florida (June, 1995).

BOTTOM: Clay and Kim with Disney's Chip 'n Dale in Orlando, Florida -- at breakfast with the characters in June, 1995.

ROS & RICH DALRYMPLE

PERSONAL DATA

BORN: *Rich* -- 8-2-60 in Pittsburgh, Pennsylvania; *Ros* -- 1-10-64 in Cape Town, South Africa

COLLEGE: *Rich* -- Westminster College - Pennsylvania; *Ros* -- University of Miami (Public Relations)

FAVORITE ACADEMIC SUBJECT: *Rich* -- History; *Ros* -- Public Relations

WIFE'S OCCUPATION: Housewife and part-time tennis teaching pro

FAVORITE TYPE OF MUSIC: *Rich* -- Soft rock, Jackson Browne and Bob Segar; *Ros* -- Classic rock

FAVORITE FOOD: *Rich* -- Healthy Mexican; *Ros* -- Sauteed vegetables

FAVORITE AUTHOR: *Rich* -- Frank DeFord; *Ros* -- Ken Follet and children's development books

FAVORITE SPORTS HERO: *Rich* -- Roberto Clemente; *Ros* -- Chris Evert

HOBBIES AND INTERESTS: *Rich* -- Working around the house; *Ros* -- Tennis, golf, and raising children

HOW MET: Met, when sports information director at the University of Miami, while covering women's tennis

CHILDREN AND AGES: Kimberley Rose - 3-1/2 yrs.; Clayton James - 20 months

PET PEEVE: Waiting in traffic

FITNESS AND DIET TIP: Eat balanced meals of acidic and alkaline foods for better digestion and food distribution, use fresh vegetables, and have some type of work-out program

Clay and Kim with "Tiggr" at Disney World in Orlando, Florida --
at breakfast with the characters in June, 1995.

ROS & RICH DALRYMPLE

PROFESSIONAL DATA

Director of Public Relations

YEARS IN PROFESSIONAL FOOTBALL: Six years

FIRST PLAYED ORGANIZED FOOTBALL: In seventh grade

GREATEST MOMENT IN SPORTS: Watching the Dallas Cowboys win the 1992 NFC Championship game

HONORS OR AWARDS: *Ros* -- Professional tennis ranking #288 (1983); All-America (1984-1986)

TOP: Jim and Sharlene Eddy -- on their wedding day (6-17-95) in Dallas.

BOTTOM: Sharlene and Jim at Pro Bowl party in Hawaii in February, 1995.

SHARLENE & JIM EDDY

PERSONAL DATA

BORN: *Jim* -- 5-2-39 in Checotah, Oklahoma; *Sharlene* -- 7-22-68 in Norman, Oklahoma

COLLEGE: *Jim* -- New Mexico State University (B.A. and M.A.); *Sharlene* -- University of Oklahoma (B.A. -- Business Marketing)

FAVORITE ACADEMIC SUBJECT: *Jim* -- Psychology; *Sharlene* -- Business Economics

WIFE'S OCCUPATION: Financial Account Specialist/Consultant -- AT & T Global Information Solutions, Systemedia Division

FAVORITE TYPE OF MUSIC: *Jim* -- Country; *Sharlene* -- All types

FAVORITE FOOD: *Jim* -- Anything chocolate and Mexican; *Sharlene* -- All types of pasta and Mexican

FAVORITE AUTHOR: *Jim* and *Sharlene* -- John Grisham

FAVORITE SPORTS HERO: *Jim* -- Johnny Unitas; *Sharlene* -- Nolan Ryan

HOBBIES AND INTERESTS: *Jim* -- Raising and training horses, fishing, woodworking, skiing, and traveling; *Sharlene* -- Running, skiing, painting, traveling, reading, and gardening

CHILDREN AND AGES: *Jim* -- Kelley Kathleen Tobin - 32 yrs.; and Connie Irene Eddy - 31 yrs.; Jim and *Sharlene* -- Expecting first child in March, 1996

FITNESS AND DIET TIP: Move -- do anything that gets you moving; try to integrate your interests into your exercise method; and change your exercise routine often to keep it interesting and keep you involved

LONG-RANGE CAREER GOAL: To be a head coach in the NFL

Sharlene and Jim Eddy (July, 1995).

JIM EDDY

PROFESSIONAL DATA

ASSISTANT COACH
Linebackers

FIRST PLAYED ORGANIZED FOOTBALL: As a freshman running back for the Checotah (Oklahoma) High School "Wildcats"

YEARS IN PROFESSIONAL FOOTBALL: Sixteen years; 3rd season with the Dallas Cowboys

EXPERIENCE, HONORS, AND AWARDS: For ten seasons, including three as head coach, worked in the Canadian Football League (CFL), where his teams made eight post-season berths and played in four Grey Cup Championship games; during three seasons with the Houston Oilers, team earned three playoff berths, including the franchise's first AFC Central Division crown; in 1991, guided the Oilers defense, which led the AFC; in 1992, finished third in the NFL in total defense; in 1993 -- his first year with the Dallas Cowboys -- added defensive knowledge and experience to help land three Cowboys' defenders in the Pro Bowl; in 1994, moved from the secondary to the linebackers, aiding three starting linebackers to record career highs for tackles

Janice and Robert Ford -- enjoying dinner at John Dominis in Hawaii in February, 1995, while at the Pro Bowl.

JANICE AND ROBERT FORD

PERSONAL DATA

BORN: *Robert* -- 6-21-51 in Belton, Texas; *Janice* -- 4-8-54 in Saginaw, Michigan

HIGH SCHOOL: *Robert* -- Belton High School in Texas

COLLEGE: *Robert* -- University of Houston (B.S. -- Education) and Western Illinois University (M.A. -- Athletic Administration; *Janice* -- Delta College

WIFE'S OCCUPATION: Being the best mom and wife possible

FAVORITE TYPE OF MUSIC: *Robert* -- "Good music" that he can sing (ha! ha!) and dance to (does not include rap or country); *Janice* -- Rhythm and blues, and jazz

FAVORITE FOOD: *Robert* -- Banana pudding, and chicken and pineapple stir-fry over rice; *Janice* -- Most pastas and Mexican food

FAVORITE AUTHOR: *Robert* -- John Grisham and Michael Crichton; *Janice* -- John Grisham and Tom Clancy

FAVORITE SPORTS HERO: *Robert* -- Lenny Moore; *Janice* -- Jim Thorpe and Jackie Robinson

HOBBIES AND INTERESTS: *Robert* -- Golf, reading, bowling, and jet skiing; *Janice* -- Bowling, football, and reading

CHILDREN AND AGES: Bobby - 20 yrs. (junior at Texas A & M University); and Jason - 17 yrs. (senior at Coppell High School)

PETS: A little white dog with the cutest face ever -- "Frostie" (Bichon Frise)

FITNESS AND DIET TIP: Walk 45 minutes every day; eat bananas; don't overeat -- when you're full, stop; and never eat after 7 p.m.

TOP: Jason Ford in spring, 1994, on an estate in Fort Worth *(photographed by Smiley's)*.

BOTTOM: Bobby Ford, taken on an estate in Fort Worth in the spring of 1994, *(photographed by Smiley's)*.

ROBERT L. FORD

PROFESSIONAL DATA

ASSISTANT COACH
Tight Ends

FIRST PLAYED ORGANIZED FOOTBALL: When twelve years old as a running back and guard for the Smith Street "Bears"

YEARS IN PROFESSIONAL FOOTBALL: 4th season with the Dallas Cowboys

ENJOY MOST ABOUT BEING WITH THE DALLAS COWBOYS: "Winning!" The camaraderie and fellowship of working with the other coaches; most of all, being able to teach the young guys "a thing or two about football"

EXPERIENCE, HONORS, AND AWARDS: Only player in history of the NCAA to catch two 99-yd. touchdown passes; in 1972, led University of Houston in receiving, punt returns, and kickoff returns, earning third-team All-America honors; College Hall of Fame finalist; began coaching career at Saginaw, Michigan, in 1973; moved on as receivers coach at Western Illinois (1974-1976), New Mexico (1977-1979), Oregon State (1980-1981), Mississippi State (1982-1983), and Kansas (1986); receivers coach with the Houston Gamblers in 1985; as receivers coach at Texas A & M, spent 1989-1990 helping the Aggies to two Bowl appearances; first full-time assignment with Dallas Cowboys in 1991 -- his first season coaching tight ends; since 1990, including four seasons under Ford, no other NFL tight end has caught more passes than Novacek's 277; in 1992, Novacek hauled in more passes than any other tight end in Cowboys' history; in 1993, while coaching the tight ends -- Novacek made his third consecutive Pro Bowl appearance, and was named the 1993 NFL Alumni Tight End of the Year Award; in 1994, Novacek was named to his fourth straight Pro Bowl after recording 47 catches for 475 yards -- his reception and yard totals ranked second in the NFC for receptions in a season

Steve and Raffy Hoffman in 1994.

RAFFY & STEVE HOFFMAN

PERSONAL DATA

BORN: *Steve* -- 9-8-58 in Camden, New Jersey; Raffaella (*Raffy*) -- 9-23-66 in Milan, Italy

HIGH SCHOOL: *Steve* -- York Suburban High School in York, Pennsylvania

COLLEGE: *Steve* -- Dickinson College (B.A. -- Economics) and St. Thomas University (M.A. -- Sports Administration; *Raffy* -- Oxford Institute of Languages - Monza, Italy

WIFE'S OCCUPATION: International flight attendant

FAVORITE TYPE OF MUSIC: *Steve* -- "Anything but bad jazz"; *Raffy* -- Club music . . . also soul and good country

FAVORITE FOOD: *Steve* -- Pasta; *Raffy* -- Pasta and Mexican

FAVORITE AUTHOR: *Steve* -- Leon Uris, Joseph Wambaugh, and James Clavell; *Raffy* -- Alberto Bevilacqua and Fracesco Alberoni

FAVORITE SPORTS HERO: *Steve* -- Ed Podolak; *Raffy* -- Roberto Baggio

HOBBIES AND INTERESTS: *Steve* -- Reading, studying Italian, listening to music, and watching old movies; *Raffy* -- Sewing, decorating, reading, dancing, and cooking

CHILDREN AND AGES: Expecting first baby - due in October, 1995

PETS: Six-year-old Maltese - "Pongo"

FITNESS AND DIET TIP: Vary your workouts so you don't get bored; and marry an Italian -- eat pasta with every meal!

TOP: Raffy and Steve Hoffman.

BOTTOM: Raffy and Steve in Italy during a vacation.

STEVE HOFFMAN

PROFESSIONAL DATA

ASSISTANT COACH
Kickers / Quality Control

FIRST PLAYED ORGANIZED FOOTBALL: In 1966, when eight years old, as running back with the East York County Boys Club (Pennsylvania)

YEARS IN PROFESSIONAL FOOTBALL: 7th season with the Dallas Cowboys

ENJOY MOST ABOUT BEING WITH THE DALLAS COWBOYS: Having the chance every week to be a part of something most people can only dream about

EXPERIENCE, HONORS, AND AWARDS: Starred in baseball and football at York Suburban High School; earned All-Mid-Atlantic Conference honors in football in 1978-1979; All-Mid-Atlantic Conference honors in baseball in 1979 and 1980; joined Dallas Cowboys in 1989 to coach the kickers; received added duties of quality control in 1990; currently, coordinates the computer scouting of all of the Cowboys' future opponents on video tape, while providing internal analysis of the Cowboys' own tendencies and productivity; has rapidly developed a reputation around the NFL for his ability to find and develop kicking talents with young players; in 1993, introduced free agent punter John Jett to the NFL -- Jett responded by finishing ranked third in NFL in net punting average (37.7) in 1993; in 1994, found free agent Chris Boniol, and the place kicker went on to hit 22-of-29 field goal attempts and finished the season third in the NFC in scoring with 114 points; in four of the last five seasons, Hoffman has developed a rookie free agent kicker or punter who has become a productive performer as a Dallas Cowboys' starter

Elsie and Hudson Houck with Hudson's mother, Lucille.

ELSIE & HUDSON HOUCK

PERSONAL DATA

BORN: *Hudson* -- 1-7-43 in Los Angeles, California; *Elsie* -- 12-22-47 in Rochester, Pennsylvania

HIGH SCHOOL: *Hudson* -- Eagle Rock High School in Los Angeles, California

COLLEGE: *Hudson* -- University of Southern California (Education); *Elsie* -- University of Virginia (Bank Management)

WIFE'S OCCUPATION: Regional Manager for Bank One

FAVORITE TYPE OF MUSIC: *Hudson* -- Jazz and country western; *Elsie* -- Oldies and Country/western

FAVORITE FOOD: *Hudson* and *Elsie* -- Mexican

FAVORITE AUTHOR: *Hudson* -- John Grisham; *Elsie* -- Sidney Sheldon

FAVORITE SPORTS HERO: *Hudson* -- Vince Lombardi

HOBBIES AND INTERESTS: *Hudson* -- Golf, snow skiing, and fishing; *Elsie* -- Golf, snow skiing, scuba diving, and travel

CHILDREN AND AGES: Troy - 31 yrs.; Scott - 26 yrs.; and Holly - 23 yrs.

FITNESS AND DIET TIP: Walk four miles every day, eliminate fat from the diet, and drink plenty of water

Holly, Scott, and Elsie's mother, Sarah.

HUDSON HOUCK

PROFESSIONAL DATA

ASSISTANT COACH
Offensive Line

FIRST PLAYED ORGANIZED FOOTBALL: In 1957, played linebacker/fullback for the Eagle Rock "Eagles" in Los Angeles

YEARS IN PROFESSIONAL FOOTBALL: Los Angeles Rams - 9 yrs.; Seattle Seahawks - 1 yr.; and in 3rd season with the Dallas Cowboys

EXPERIENCE, HONORS, AND AWARDS: Played three seasons as a center for the University of Southern California -- including being on the Trojans' 1962 National Championship team; in the nine years with the Los Angeles Rams, developed one of the most dominate lines in the NFL -- no team sent more offensive lineman to the Pro Bowl than the Rams; in first season in Dallas (1993), helped guide three members of the offensive line to the Pro Bowl; in 1994, his group established club records by allowing just 20 sacks for losses, totaling 93 yards -- the fewest number of sack yards given up in the League last year (on 448 passing attempts, one per every 22.4 pass attempts); Nate Newton, Mark Stepnoski, and Mark Tuinei were chosen to participate in the Pro Bowl in 1994, marking the second straight season Dallas has had three offensive linemen in Hawaii for the game; Houck, in just two seasons, has molded the Cowboys' offensive line into one of the top units in club history

Larry and Criss Lacewell in Destin, Florida -- a favorite vacation
spot.

CRISS & LARRY LACEWELL

PERSONAL DATA

BORN: *Larry* -- 2-12-37 in Fordyce, Arkansas; *Criss* -- 12-14-43 in Indianapolis, Indiana

HIGH SCHOOL: *Larry* -- Fordyce High School in Fordyce, Arkansas

COLLEGE: *Larry* -- Arkansas A & M - Monticello, Arkansas (B.A.) and University of Alabama (M.S.); *Criss* -- Butler University - Indianapolis (B.A. -- Sociology); Indiana University (M.S. -- Secondary Education); and Arkansas State University (Ed.S. -- Student Personnel Services)

FAVORITE ACADEMIC SUBJECT: *Larry* -- History; *Criss* -- Psychology and Sociology

WIFE'S OCCUPATION: Elementary guidance counselor for twelve years (currently, Coppell I.S.D. - 4 years); previously, a real estate broker

FAVORITE TYPE OF MUSIC: *Larry* -- Golden oldies (Frank Sinatra); *Criss* -- Duke Ellington, 50's and 60's rock and roll, and Willie Nelson

FAVORITE FOOD: *Larry* -- Pasta, turnip greens, and any South Arkansas home cooking; *Criss* -- Sushi, Chinese, and Cajun

FAVORITE AUTHOR: *Larry* -- Historical and sports biographies; *Criss* -- Willie Morris and Mary Higgins Clark

FAVORITE SPORTS HERO: *Larry* -- Bear Bryant; *Criss* -- Branch McCracken, long-time Indiana basketball coach

HOBBIES AND INTERESTS: *Larry* -- Golf, reading biographies, fishing, and more golf; *Criss* -- Baking bread, crossword puzzles, reading, herb garden, and beach in Destin, Florida

CHILDREN AND AGES: Bryant Layne - 23 yrs. (Dallas Art Institute); and Logan Cross - 14 yrs. (8th grade in Coppell)

PETS: Pit Bulls - "Sunshine" and "Clara Belle"

Larry, Logan, Criss, and Layne -- at a Cowboys' game in Dallas.

LARRY LACEWELL

PROFESSIONAL DATA

Director of College and Pro Scouting

FIRST PLAYED ORGANIZED FOOTBALL: In junior high played halfback for the Fordyce (Arkansas) Red Bugs; was known as "Baby Bugs"

YEARS IN PROFESSIONAL FOOTBALL: 3-1/2 years with the Dallas Cowboys

GREATEST MOMENT IN SPORTS: Both Super Bowls with the Cowboys

EXPERIENCE, HONORS, AND AWARDS: Played halfback at Arkansas A & M from 1955-1959; began coaching career as an assistant at Alabama in 1959; moved to Arkansas State (1961), Arkansas A & M (1962-1963), Kilgore Junior College (1964-1965), Oklahoma (1966), Wichita State (1967), and Iowa State (1968); rejoined the Sooners' staff in 1969 as assistant head coach and defensive coordinator; over the next nine seasons helped Oklahoma to six Big Eight titles and two national championships; as athletic director and head coach at Arkansas State (1978-1989), compiled a record of 69-48-4; named the Southland Conference's Coach of the year on three occasions, while the Indians captured two conference titles under his direction; joined the Cowboys as Director of College Scouting in 1992 and coordinated the Cowboys' effort in the 1993-1995 NFL Drafts; in 1994, was charged with the additional responsibility of overseeing pro personnel; now directs the Cowboys' personnel evaluation for all college prospects, as well as the NFL's other 29 teams and the newly-restructured World League

Jim and Rosanne Maurer at the Pro Bowl in Honolulu, Hawaii --
just arriving at the hotel!

ROSANNE & JIM MAURER

PERSONAL DATA

BORN: *Jim* -- 3-8-65 in Dallas, Texas; *Rosanne* -- 2-23-65 in Dallas, Texas

COLLEGE: *Jim* -- Southern Methodist University (B.A. -- Physical Education); *Rosanne* -- Texas Tech

WIFE'S OCCUPATION: Sells and coordinates product workshops for Sterling Software in Las Colinas

FAVORITE FOOD: *Jim* -- Barbecue ribs; *Rosanne* -- Anything Italian

FAVORITE SPORTS HERO: *Jim* -- Walter Payton; *Rosanne* -- Bill Bates

HOBBIES AND INTERESTS: *Jim* -- Golf and racquetball; *Rosanne* -- Reading (fiction and non-fiction); and speaking in toastmasters' group, Las Colinas Communicators

CHILDREN AND AGES: Nicholas "Nick" - 6-1/2 yrs.; and Benjamin Michael "Ben" - 3 yrs.

FITNESS AND DIET TIP: *Jim* -- Consistent, slow progression when using weight programs, and look into a lifestyle change rather than a quick-fix diet; Rosanne -- Get in touch with your body . . . and then listen to it!

LONG-RANGE CAREER GOAL: *Jim* -- To be a head trainer in a professional athletic setting; *Rosanne* -- To be a motivational speaker, training speakers and sales professionals

Rosanne, Nick, Jim, and Ben -- at Fort Worth Botanical Gardens
(Diane Watts Photography).

JIM MAURER

PROFESSIONAL DATA

Assistant Athletic Trainer

YEARS IN PROFESSIONAL FOOTBALL: Joined the Dallas Cowboys on a full-time basis in the spring of 1990

ENJOY MOST ABOUT BEING WITH THE DALLAS COWBOYS: Helping athletes in the rehabilitative process after an injury; and making friends

EXPERIENCE: Worked primarily with the football and swim teams while earning undergraduate degree from Southern Methodist University; worked one year as a summer assistant with the Kansas City Chiefs in 1987, after spending the summer of 1986 with the Cowboys in the same capacity; works with Kevin O'Neill and supervises the Cowboys' medical rehabilitation program; after serving as a graduate assistant with Dallas for two seasons, then joined the Cowboys on a full-time basis

TOP: Bruce and Kathy Mays -- at a dinner party for Christmas Neiman-Marcus trip.

BOTTOM: Sisters -- Laura and Jennifer Ingle -- hugging at home in Coppell.

KATHY & BRUCE B. MAYS

PERSONAL DATA

FRONT OFFICE STAFF
Director of Operations

BORN: *Bruce* -- 8-16-43 in Cleveland, Ohio; *Kathryn (Kathy)* -- 1-6-48 in Detroit, Michigan

COLLEGE: *Bruce* -- Ohio Northern University (B.S. -- Education); University of Akron (M.S. -- Education); Oklahoma State University (Course work completed for Doctorate in Higher Education and Administration); *Kathy* -- Oklahoma State University (B.S. and M.S.)

ENJOY MOST ABOUT BEING WITH THE DALLAS COWBOYS: Being associated with the players and staff of the Dallas Cowboys

WIFE'S OCCUPATION: Registered Dietitian at Cooper Clinic -- Cooper Aerobic Center in Dallas

FAVORITE TYPE OF MUSIC: *Bruce* -- Opera; *Kathy* -- Classical piano

FAVORITE FOOD: *Bruce* -- Italian, Mexican, and Chinese; *Kathy* -- Seafood, Italian, and Oriental

FAVORITE AUTHOR: *Bruce* -- Ernest Hemingway; *Kathy* -- Michael Crichton

FAVORITE SPORTS HERO: *Bruce* -- Ted Williams; *Kathy* -- Bobby Richardson

HOBBIES AND INTERESTS: *Bruce* -- Reading, golf, and running; *Kathy* -- Reading, attending musicals, and visiting museums and art galleries

CHILDREN AND AGES: Kirsten - 26 yrs.; Jennifer - 20 yrs.; Laura - 18 yrs.; and Damien - 18 yrs.

PETS: Toy Poodle - "Shakespeare"

FITNESS AND DIET TIP: Exercise consistently three to five days per week for 30 to 45 minutes -- include three days of aerobics; cut the fat -- increase the carbohydrates; and eat a wide variety of foods

Jan and Mike McCord.

JAN & MIKE McCORD

PERSONAL DATA

BORN: *Mike* – 11-6-64 in Clovis, New Mexico; Jan – 2-20-63 in Dimmitt, Texas

HIGH SCHOOL: *Mike* – Roosevelt High School in San Antonio, Texas

COLLEGE: *Mike* – Southwest Texas State (for 2 yrs.); transferred to University of Texas - Austin (B.B.A. -- Business Administration and Marketing); *Jan* – West Texas State University (B.A. – Agri-Business)

WIFE'S OCCUPATION: Bookkeeper for Oppel Jenkins Homes

FAVORITE TYPE OF MUSIC: *Mike* and *Jan* – Country

FAVORITE FOOD: *Mike* – Italian; *Jan* – Mexican

FAVORITE AUTHOR: *Mike* – James Michener; *Jan* – John Grisham

FAVORITE SPORTS HERO: *Mike* – Mike Schmidt; *Jan* – Troy Aikman

HOBBIES AND INTERESTS: *Mike* -- Golf, basketball, baseball, tennis, movies, country dancing, and spending time working in the yard; *Jan* – Water skiing, dancing, antiques, and decorating new home

PETS: Dogs – "Jasper" and "Sheeba"

TOP: Jan and Mike McCord at a Christmas party.

BOTTOM: Jan and Mike -- at Mark Tuinei's Hawaiian luau and golf tournament while at Pro Bowl in February, 1995.

MIKE McCORD

PROFESSIONAL DATA

Equipment Manager

YEARS IN PROFESSIONAL FOOTBALL: 7th season with the Dallas Cowboys -- 4th in the Equipment Department, and 2nd as the Equipment Manager

ENJOY MOST ABOUT BEING WITH THE DALLAS COWBOYS: The relationships that are formed with the guys who have the same commitment to winning

EXPERIENCE: Before coming to Dallas, spent 2-1/2 years with the University of Texas Athletic Department -- 1-1/2 years as a part-time student assistant before receiving B.B.A. degree, and then, one year as a full-time intern; originally joined the Cowboys in 1989 as the assistant ticket manager, spending two years in that capacity before moving to the Football Operations Department in 1991

Anne and Kevin O'Neill -- vacationing in St. Martine in the French West Indies.

ANNE & KEVIN O'NEILL

PERSONAL DATA

BORN: *Kevin* -- 8-2-54 in Pittsburgh, Pennsylvania; *Anne* -- 12-26-? in Los Angeles, California

COLLEGE: *Kevin* -- University of Pittsburgh (B.S. -- Physical Education) and University of Arizona (M.S. -- Athletic Training); *Anne* -- Oregon State University (B.S. -- Home Economics)

FAVORITE FOOD: *Kevin* -- Italian; *Anne* -- Anything chocolate

FAVORITE AUTHOR: *Kevin* -- John Grisham

HOBBIES AND INTERESTS: *Kevin* -- Jogging, movies, and spending most of free time with daughters; *Anne* -- Loves to travel

CHILDREN AND AGES: McKenzie Jean - 10 yrs.; and Kaitlyn Elizabeth - 9 yrs.

PETS: Beagles - "Daisy" and "Dixie"

FITNESS AND DIET TIP: Make sure you select a proper-fitting pair of running/workout shoes, and eat five servings of fruits and vegetables a day for better health

SPECIAL COMMENTS: Being involved with football has given us the opportunity to live in many different places, having met the most wonderful people at each place; feel very fortunate to have had a tremendous amount of success -- including a National Championship and two Super Bowl titles

McKenzie and Kaitlyn on Baie Longue in St. Martine.

KEVIN P. O'NEILL

PROFESSIONAL DATA

Head Athletic Trainer

YEARS IN PROFESSIONAL FOOTBALL: 6th season with the Dallas Cowboys

ENJOY MOST ABOUT BEING WITH THE DALLAS COWBOYS: Camaraderie of working with the staff, coaches, and players

EXPERIENCE, HONORS, AND AWARDS: Served as athletic trainer for Catalina High School in Tucson, Arizona, while earning Master's degree in physical education; spent three years as the assistant athletic trainer at the University of Tennessee, four years as head athletic trainer at Oregon State, and one year at the University of Central Florida, before joining the University of Miami; served four years as head athletic trainer at the University of Miami; joined the Dallas Cowboys in 1989; serves as chairman of the public relations committee for the National Athletic Trainers Association

TOP: Mike Woicik -- a big catch!

BOTTOM: Mike at Pro Bowl.

MIKE WOICIK

PERSONAL and PROFESSIONAL DATA

FRONT OFFICE STAFF
Director of Operations

BORN: 9-26-56 in Baltimore, Maryland

HIGH SCHOOL: Westwood High School, Massachusetts

COLLEGE: Boston College (B.A. -- History) and Springfield College (M.A. -- Physical Education)

YEARS IN PROFESSIONAL FOOTBALL: 5th season with the Dallas Cowboys

ENJOY MOST ABOUT BEING WITH THE DALLAS COWBOYS: The players with whom I work

EXPERIENCE, HONORS, AND AWARDS: Competed in football and track in high school; outstanding discus thrower at Boston College, setting school record of 180 feet, 5 inches; earned All-East honors and qualified for NCAA championships; came to Cowboys after serving 10 years as strength and conditioning coach at Syracuse University, which became one of the nation's top football programs during his tenure; named NFL Strength Coach of the Year in 1992 (as voted by peers); developed Dallas Cowboys into one of the healthiest and best-conditioned teams in NFL; since coming to Dallas in 1990, has an overall record of 63-27, with eight playoff victories and two Super Bowl titles; has conditioned Cowboys so well in each of the past four seasons, that Dallas has cumulative record of 25-7 in games played from Thanksgiving on through to the end of playoffs

FAVORITE TYPE OF MUSIC: Doo wop, rhythm and blues, and oldies

FAVORITE FOOD: Prime rib at Paul's Porterhouse

FAVORITE AUTHOR: Robert Ludlum

FAVORITE SPORTS HERO: Willie Mays

HOBBIES AND INTERESTS: Bowling, fishing, reading, music, and golf

Zampese family: Children and grandchildren in Coppell (7-95).

JOYCE & ERNIE ZAMPESE

PERSONAL DATA

BORN: *Ernie* -- 3-12-36 in Santa Barbara, California; *Joyce* -- 11-23-35 in Chicago, Illinois

HIGH SCHOOL: *Ernie* and *Joyce* -- Santa Barbara High School in California

COLLEGE: *Ernie* -- University of Southern California - Cal Poly - San Luis Obispo (B.A. and M.A. -- Education); *Joyce* -- Marymount College - Westwood - Cal Poly - U.C.S.B. - San Luis Obispo (B.A. and M.A. -- Education)

FAVORITE ACADEMIC SUBJECT: *Ernie* -- Biology; *Joyce* -- Merchandising and Psychology

FAVORITE FOOD: *Ernie* -- Steak; *Joyce* -- Buttered popcorn

FAVORITE AUTHOR: *Ernie* -- Louis L'Amour; *Joyce* -- Taylor Caldwell

FAVORITE SPORTS HERO: *Ernie* -- Joe DiMaggio; *Joyce* -- Husband Ernie

HONORS OR AWARDS: *Joyce* -- Santa Barbara High School Homecoming Queen, Marymount College Freshman Class Queen, and Loyola University Homecoming Queen

CHILDREN AND AGES: Kristin - 33 yrs.; Laurie - 31 yrs.; Ken - 28 yrs.; and Joe - 20 yrs.

GRANDCHILDREN AND AGES: Jillean - 10 yrs.; Boone - 8 yrs.; Chelsey - 6 yrs.; Jesse - 4 yrs.; and Jenna - 4 yrs.

FITNESS AND DIET TIP: Walking . . . and don't over-indulge!

Celebrating son Ken's and wife Christine's anniversary in Texas in July, 1995.

ERNIE ZAMPESE

PROFESSIONAL DATA

ASSISTANT COACH
Offensive Coordinator

FIRST PLAYED ORGANIZED FOOTBALL: As tailback for Santa Barbara (California) Dons in 1951

EXPERIENCE, HONORS, AND AWARDS: High School Player of the Year in Southern California in 1953; began coaching career at Allan Hancock Junior College in Santa Maria, California; then, coached at Cal Poly-SLO in 1966, before moving to San Diego State from 1967-1975, where he coached defensive backs; began pro coaching career as a defensive backs coach for the San Diego Chargers in 1976; in 1977, became a scout for the New York Jets; returned to the Chargers in 1979; served as the Chargers wide receivers coach from 1979-1982; offensive coordinator for San Diego from 1983-1986; joined the Los Angeles Rams' staff in 1987, serving seven seasons with the Rams (1987-1993); in twelve years as an offensive coordinator, Zampese's teams have ranked in the top five in total offense six times; joined the Dallas Cowboys in 1994, with the Dallas offense finishing the year eighth in the NFL in total offense with 332.6 yards per game -- Cowboys were second in scoring with 25.9 points per game (the Cowboys' best scoring output since 1983); Zampese's offensive team was fueled by Emmitt Smith, who led the NFL and set a club record with 22 touchdowns, and Troy Aikman, who completed 64.5% of his passes and set a new club record with the highest attempts per sack ratio ever (25.8); the Cowboys' offensive line allowed Dallas to snap the club record for fewest sacks in a season, allowing just 20 sacks in the year

TOP: Zimmer family -- vacationing in Florida (July, 1995).

BOTTOM: Daddy's girls -- at the Pro Bowl in Hawaii.

VIKKI & MIKE ZIMMER

PERSONAL DATA

BORN: *Mike* -- 6-5-56 in Peoria, Illinois; *Vikki* -- 6-9-59

HIGH SCHOOL: *Mike* -- Lockport (Illinois) High School

COLLEGE: *Mike* -- Illinois State University (B.A. -- Physical Education); *Vikki* -- Weber State / University of Utah (Degree in Dance)

FAVORITE TYPE OF MUSIC: *Mike* -- Country; *Vikki* -- All types

FAVORITE FOOD: *Mike* -- Mexican; *Vikki* -- Shrimp

FAVORITE AUTHOR: *Vikki* -- Helen Steiner Rice

FAVORITE SPORTS HERO: *Mike* -- Joe Namath; *Vikki* -- Mike and his dad, Bill

HOBBIES AND INTERESTS: *Mike* -- Hunting, fishing, and racquetball; *Vikki* -- Dance, judging pageants and competitions and cheerleaders, cooking, crafts, homemaking, and love people

HONORS OR AWARDS: *Vikki* -- Miss Weber State College; dance instructor for 21 years; member of Ballet West Co.; Weber State cheerleader for 3 years; U.S.A. cheerleader; Mrs. Layton, Utah, in 1979

CHILDREN AND AGES: Adam William - 11-1/2 yrs.; Marki Nichole - 8-1/2 yrs.; and Corri Dawn - 5-1/2 yrs.

PETS: Yellow Lab - "Hunter"; and floppy-eared bunny - "Sniffles"

FITNESS AND DIET TIP: Get in a routine and vary exercises to keep interesting, cut out the fat, and work out

Adam -- on his championship team, the "Yankees", in 1995.

MIKE ZIMMER

PROFESSIONAL DATA

ASSISTANT COACH
Defensive Backs

FIRST PLAYED ORGANIZED FOOTBALL: In sixth grade for the Kelvin Grove "Hornets"

ENJOY MOST ABOUT BEING WITH THE DALLAS COWBOYS: New lifelong friendships with genuine people!

EXPERIENCE, HONORS, AND AWARDS: Two-time All-Conference quarterback at Lockport (Illinois) High School; also earned All-Conference honors in wrestling and baseball; quarterback and linebacker at Illinois State University; began coaching career as a part-time assistant on defense at University of Missouri in 1979; assistant at Weber State College from 1981-1988 -- coached inside linebackers from 1981-1984, adding the duties of defensive coordinator in 1983; from 1985-1988, served as coordinator and oversaw the secondary; the 1981 Wildcat defense led the Big Sky Conference, and Zimmer's 1987 group set a school record with six defensive touchdowns -- 1987 team had the best record in school history (10-3); spent five seasons as the defensive coordinator/secondary coach at Washington State University; coached best defense in school history at Washington State (1992-1993); in 1993, Washington State climbed to eighth in the nation in total defense and second in rushing defense; coached Blue-Grey All-Star Game in 1993; joined Dallas Cowboys in 1994, taking over the responsibility for a secondary that helped the Cowboys' defense finish the season as the top-ranked pass defense in the League; Zimmer inherits a secondary that was part of NFL's top-ranked defense in 1994

COOKBOOK
"FAVORITE RECIPES"

Spinach Dip

(Jason Garrett)

2 packages frozen, chopped spinach (10-ounce package)
1 package Knorr vegetable soup mix
1 container light sour cream (16 ounces)
1 cup light mayonnaise
1 can sliced water chestnuts, chopped (8 ounces)
5 scallions (green onions), chopped
1 package King Hawaiian bread
1 bag tortilla chips

Thaw spinach; squeeze dry. Combine soup mix, sour cream, and mayonnaise. Stir in spinach, chopped water chestnuts, and chopped scallions. Chill in the refrigerator for 2 hours. Cut out the center of bread; serve spinach dip in center. Cut up remaining bread into pieces; use bread and/or tortilla chips for dipping.

Maribeth Rodee Dip

(Ernie Zampese)

1 cup mayonnaise
green onions, chopped
1 cup grated Cheddar cheese
3 to 4 dashes Worcestershire sauce
Triscuits

Mix all ingredients together. Spread on Triscuits. Put in 350-degree oven until brown. Serve on plate or tray.

Hudson's Salmon Pate

(HUDSON HOUCK)

1 can red salmon, drained (1 pound)
1 package cream cheese (8 ounces)
1 tablespoon lemon juice
2 tablespoons grated onion
1 tablespoon horseradish
1/4 teaspoon salt
1/4 teaspoon liquid smoke

Mix ingredients together; refrigerate overnight. Serve as an appetizer with crackers.

Cheesy Hot Quiche Squares

(DIXON EDWARDS)

8 eggs
1/2 cup all-purpose flour
1 teaspoon baking powder
3/4 teaspoon salt
4 cups shredded Monterey Jack cheese
1-1/2 cups cottage cheese
1/4 cup chopped jalapeno peppers

Beat eggs 3 minutes. Combine flour, baking powder, and salt. Add to eggs; mix well. Stir in cheese and peppers. Pour into a greased 13" x 9" x 2" baking pan; bake at 350 degrees for 30 to 35 minutes. Let cool for 10 minutes; cut into squares. Makes 12 servings.

Diana's Crepes Fruits de Mer

(DIANA BLACKWELL)

This is a centuries-old classic French recipe. Flaked crab meat, or fish, is added for textural contrast to the shrimp and oysters. Fill the crepes generously with the seafood mixture, fold over to make half-moon shapes, and serve garnished with broiled tomatoes.

4 tablespoons unsalted butter (1/2 stick)
1/4 cup all-purpose flour
2 cups "Seafood Stock" *
1 pound raw shrimp, peeled and deveined
4 cloves of garlic, minced
2 bay leaves
2 cups heavy cream
2 tablespoons paprika
1/2 cup dry sherry
1 cup coarsely-chopped green onion tops
1 pound flaked lump crab meat, shells carefully removed
   -- or non-oily fish   (2 cups)
24 oysters
salt and freshly-ground black pepper
8 "crepes"

Melt butter in a small saucepan. Stir in flour; cook the blond roux until smooth and bubbling. Set aside. In a 2-quart saucepan, bring the seafood stock to a boil. Add shrimp; return to the boil. Reduce heat; simmer until shrimp are cooked (approximately 5 minutes). Add garlic and bay leaves; gradually stir in cream and paprika. Simmer for 3 to 4 minutes. Add roux; stir until sauce is smooth and thickened. Add sherry, green onions, crab meat, oysters, and salt and pepper to taste. Simmer another minute or so; remove from heat. To serve: Put 2 heaping tablespoons of the seafood-sauce mixture on one side of each crepe; fold the other side over. Top with more seafood and sauce. Serve immediately. Serves 8 as appetizer; 4 as entree. * "Seafood Stock" (page 362); "Crepes" (page 328).

Avocado/Green Chili Dip

(KEVIN SMITH)

2 avocados, peeled and sliced (save the seeds)
1 package cream cheese, softened (8 ounces)
1 can green chilies (4 ounces)
1 can taco sauce (4 ounces)
1 tablespoon Worcestershire sauce
juice of 1 lemon
salt and pepper, to taste
dash of Tabasco

Combine all of the ingredients; puree in an electric blender. Transfer to a serving bowl. Place avocado seeds in the center of the dip until ready to serve *(this will prevent the dip from turning brown)*. Chill. Serve with corn or tortilla chips.

Refrigerated Cheese Wafers

(SANDY IRVIN)

1/2 pound grated sharp cheese
1/4 pound butter, creamed
1-1/2 cups sifted flour
heavy pinch of cayenne pepper
1/2 teaspoon salt

Cream together cheese, butter, salt and pepper. Add flour. Make into a roll. Wrap in waxed paper; put in refrigerator. Will keep at least a month. When needed, slice into thin wafers. Bake in moderate oven. A pecan half can be baked on each wafer for decoration. Makes 6 to 8 dozen.

Spicy Italian Soup

(JANICE ALLEN)

hot, or mild, bulk Italian sausage (1 pound)
3 cloves garlic, finely chopped
1/2 cup elbow macaroni, uncooked
4 cups beef broth
2 tablespoons chopped, fresh (or 2 teaspoons dried)
    chervil or basil leaves
1 medium carrot, thinly sliced (1/2 cup)
1 can Italian-style tomatoes, peeled and undrained
    (28 ounces)
1 cup sliced zucchini
grated Parmesan cheese, if desired

Cook sausage and garlic in Dutch oven over medium heat, stirring occasionally. Cook until sausage is done *(is no longer pink)*; drain well.

Stir in remaining ingredients, except for zucchini and cheese. While stirring, break up the tomatoes. Heat to boiling; reduce heat. Stir in sliced zucchini.

Cover Dutch oven. Simmer about 10 minutes. Stir occasionally, until the macaroni and vegetables are tender.

Serve with cheese, if desired.

Corn Chowder

(Mike Woicik)

4 medium fresh ears of corn, or one package frozen
   whole-kernel corn (10-ounces)
1/2 cup cubed, peeled potato
1/2 cup chopped onion
1 teaspoon instant chicken bouillon granules
1/8 teaspoon white or black pepper
1-1/2 cups skim milk
2 tablespoons nonfat dry milk powder
2 tablespoons all-purpose flour
1/4 cup skim milk
1 tablespoon cooked bacon pieces

If using fresh corn, use a sharp knife to cut off just the kernel tips from the ears of corn; then scrape cobs with the dull edge of knife *(there should be 2 cups of corn)*.

Combine fresh or frozen corn, potatoes, onions, bouillon granules, pepper, and 1/3 cup water in a large saucepan. Bring to boiling; reduce heat. Cover; simmer about 10 minutes, or until corn and potatoes are just tender, stirring occasionally. Stir in 1-1/2 cups milk.

In a small mixing bowl, stir together dry milk powder and flour. Gradually stir in 1/4 cup milk until smooth. Stir milk mixture into corn mixture. Cook, stirring until mixture is thickened and bubbly. Cook; stir for 1 minute longer.

Ladle into soup bowls. Sprinkle with bacon pieces. Makes 4 servings.

La Madeleine's Tomato-Basil Soup

(KAY CAMPO)

4 cups crushed tomatoes, fresh or canned
4 cups tomato juice, or chicken stock
12 to 14 basil leaves
1 cup cream
1/4 pound butter
salt and pepper

Combine tomatoes, juice, and basil leaves in a pot; simmer for 30 minutes. Then, puree in blender. Add cream, butter, and salt and pepper. Heat until warm. <u>Do not boil!</u>

Sausage Toad-in-the-Hole

(RICH DALRYMPLE)

1-1/2 cups flour
1-1/2 cups milk
3 eggs
pinch of salt and white pepper
4 Italian sausages (or use zucchinis)
tomatoes, sliced
hot mustard

Make batter in cuisinart by combining flour, milk, eggs, and salt and pepper; pulse. Allow to stand for 30 minutes. Heat 2 tablespoons oil in 13" x 9" pyrex dish in 425-degree oven for 10 minutes. Remove *(oil will be popping)*. Poke sausages; add to pyrex (if using zucchini, cut lengthwise, if too large). Pour batter over sausages. Bake for 20 minutes at 425 degrees. Add sliced tomato; bake another 20 minutes at 375 degrees. Serve immediately with hot mustard.

Minestrone

(Dave Lang)

1/4 pound lean salt pork, finely diced
2 quarts hot water
1-1/2 cups tomato juice
2 cans kidney beans (15-ounce can)
1 can bean-with-bacon soup, undiluted (11-1/2 ounces)
6 beef bouillon cubes
1 cup diced carrot
1 cup chopped celery
1 cup shredded cabbage
1 cup chopped green onions
1 cup chopped spinach, or 1/2 package frozen, chopped
   spinach
1 teaspoon sweet basil
1/2 teaspoon salt
1/2 teaspoon freshly-ground pepper
3/4 cup uncooked regular rice
grated Parmesan cheese

Sauté salt pork in a deep saucepan until crisp and brown.
Add remaining ingredients, except rice and cheese; bring
to a boil. Cover; simmer over low heat for 1 hour, stirring
occasionally. Add rice; simmer an additional 30 minutes.

Ladle into soup bowls, and sprinkle with cheese. Makes
10 servings.

Super Supper Burgers

(Deion Sanders)

1-1/2 pounds ground beef
1 egg
1/4 cup grated carrot
1/4 cup dry bread crumbs
1 onion, chopped
1 tablespoon Worcestershire sauce
1 tablespoon dried parsley flakes
1 teaspoon salt
1/2 teaspoon poultry seasoning
1/4 teaspoon pepper
1 can tomato soup, undiluted and divided (10-3/4 ounces)
2 tablespoons vegetable oil
1 teaspoon vinegar

Combine first 10 ingredients in a large mixing bowl; mix well. Add 1/4 cup tomato soup; mix well. Shape mixture into 6 patties. In a large skillet, brown patties on both sides in hot oil. Drain off any grease.

Combine vinegar and remaining soup; stir well. Pour over burgers; bring to a boil. Reduce heat; cover and simmer for 25 minutes.

Remove cover; simmer 5 additional minutes, spooning soup over burgers occasionally. Makes 6 servings.

Ham Rolls

(ANTHONY FIELDINGS)

1/2 cup soft butter	30 slices smoked ham
2 tablespoons poppy seeds	30 slices Swiss cheese
2 teaspoons prepared mustard	30 Pepperidge Farm
1 teaspoon Worcestershire sauce	party rolls
1 small onion, grated very fine	

Mix together first 5 ingredients; spread filling on both sides of sliced party rolls. Fill rolls with a thin piece of ham and sliced Swiss cheese. Wrap with foil; heat until mixture is melted. * *These sandwiches can be frozen before heating.*

Shrimp Soup

(CAROLYN SANDERS)

2 1/2 pounds cooked shrimp	salt and pepper,
4 cups milk	to taste
1 pint cream	4 tablespoons butter
2 tablespoons flour	sherry, to taste

Clean and de-vein shrimp. Grind shrimp; add to milk. Place in top of double-boiler; cook over hot water for 30 minutes. Remove from heat; add cream, butter, flour, and salt and pepper which have been rubbed to a smooth paste. Sherry, *added just before serving*, improves the flavor. Makes 8 servings.

Michele's Pasta Salad

(BRILL ALDRIDGE-GARRETT)

1 package "Shells" pasta
1 package "Penne" pasta
1 package "Rainbow Rotini" pasta
1-1/2 cups chopped broccoli
1-1/2 cups chopped, sliced carrots
1-1/2 cups chopped cauliflower

Lawry's salt
Parmesan cheese,
  shredded
2 jars Marie's
  RanchDressing

Cook pastas, as indicated on packages; chill. Chop broccoli, carrots, and cauliflower. Mix vegetables with pastas and dressing; salt to taste. Sprinkle Parmesan cheese on top.

Apricot Salad

(JANE ARMSTRONG)

1 package apricot, or peach, jello (6 ounces)
1 can crushed pineapple (#2 can)
1 cup chopped celery
1 large package cream cheese, softened (8 ounces)
1/2 cup sugar
1 cup chopped nuts
1 quart Cool Whip

Heat pineapple and sugar to boiling; add jello. Mix thoroughly; let cool. Add cream cheese; beat. Add nuts and celery. Let stand until it starts to gel. Add Cool Whip; beat with mixer. Chill in refrigerator. Makes 8 to 10 servings.

Chinese Charred Veggie and Pasta Salad

(DARYL JOHNSTON)

1 large red pepper, sliced into 1" strips
2 medium zucchini, sliced 1/4"
2 medium yellow squash, sliced 1/4"
2 medium carrots, chopped
1 medium onion, sliced
1 bunch asparagus, chopped into 1-1/2" to 2" pieces
2 teaspoons salt
4 tablespoons low-sodium soy sauce
2 tablespoons, plus 2 teaspoons, red wine vinegar
2 teaspoons chili oil
2 teaspoons sugar
2 tablespoons peanut oil
1 package Garden Spiral pasta (12 ounces)

Layer peppers, zucchini, and squash in large bowl; sprinkle salt between layers. Let set for approximately 2 hours. Then, rinse, drain, and pat vegetables dry.
In small bowl, whisk together soy sauce, vinegar, chili oil, and sugar.

Heat a wok, or heavy skillet, over moderately-high heat until barely smoking. Add 1 tablespoon peanut oil to wok; swirl to coat. Add one-half peppers, zucchini, and squash. Cook, turning occasionally, and pressing down with wooden spatula *until nicely charred* (about 5 minutes). Transfer to bowl. Repeat procedure with the remaining peanut oil; continue with the rest of the vegetables, adding more oil if necessary. Return all vegetables to wok. Stir the reserved sauce; pour one-half over the vegetables. Cook and stir until liquid evaporates (for 1 to 2 minutes). Transfer to a large bowl. Cook pasta; drain well. Toss vegetables and pasta together with remaining liquid. Chill and serve.

Rice Salad

(ROSANNE MAURER)

1/2 cup each of carrots, cauliflower, and green beans,
    lightly steamed
4 cups cooked brown rice
1/2 cup Tamari roasted almonds
1/2 pound shellfish (shrimp or crab)
1/2 cup raw celery
1/4 cup minced parsley

Cut up and mix vegetables together. Combine all
ingredients. In separate bowl, mix dressing ingredients
well. Toss vegetables with dressing. * Best if marinated
for a few hours before serving.

Dressing:

2 tablespoons sesame oil
2 tablespoons brown rice vinegar
2 tablespoons lemon juice
1 tablespoon Tamari soy sauce
1 teaspoon oregano
2 tablespoons water
1 clove garlic
1/2 teaspoon basil
1 teaspoon oregano

Royal Salad

(JANICE MYLES)

1 can apricot halves (1-pound can)
1 package cream cheese, softened (8 ounces)
1 cup sour cream
1/4 cup sugar
1/4 teaspoon salt
1-1/2 cups pitted Bing cherries
2 cups miniature marshmallows
few drops red food coloring

Drain apricots; slice. Beat cream cheese until fluffy; stir in sour cream, sugar, and salt. Add remaining ingredients; mix well. Pour into 8-1/2" x 4-1/2" x 2-1/2" loaf pan; freeze for 6 hours, or overnight. Let stand at room temperature for several minutes; then, remove from pan. Slice; serve on crisp greens. Serves 8.

Frozen Cranberry Salad

(DOROTHY NEWTON)

1 package cream cheese (8 ounces)
3 tablespoons mayonnaise
4 tablespoons sugar
1 can crushed pineapple, drained (#2 can)
1 can cranberry sauce (16 ounces)
1 large carton whipped topping
1/2 cup chopped pecans

Cream mayonnaise and cream cheese; add sugar, pineapple, and cranberry sauce. Fold in whipped topping; add pecans. Pour into serving dish; freeze.

Eloise Lacewell's Hot Water Corn Bread

(LARRY LACEWELL)

1/3 cup Aunt Jemima's White Corn Meal *(not the self-rising kind)*

Add a lot of boiling water; stir quickly, until the consistency of mashed potatoes *(must stir a long time)*. Make oblong patties about 2 to 3 inches long (fits in the palm of your hand). Keep wetting hands with cold water to keep from sticking to the dough.

Fry in HOT grease until golden brown. Great with any South Arkansas meal!

Pork and Corn Meal Dumplings

(CRISS LACEWELL)

Cover a pork loin roast with water; boil until tender. Remove pork. Season broth with salt and pepper; add boiling broth to 2 to 3 cups Aunt Jemima's White Corn Meal *(not self-rising kind)* until the consistency of thick mashed potatoes (uses a lot of broth -- corn meal swells up with lots of stirring). Keep hands wet with cold water. Make dumplings the size of a small smashed golf ball. Return dumplings to boil in broth *at a rolling boil* for 20 to 30 minutes.

Cinnamon Raisin Bread

(Shante Carver)

1-1/2 cups milk
1/4 cup sugar
1 tablespoon salt
1/4 cup shortening
1/2 cup warm water
2 packages dry yeast
2 eggs
3 cups whole wheat flour
4-1/2 cups white flour
2 cups raisins
1-1/2 teaspoons cinnamon

Combine milk, sugar, salt, and shortening in saucepan. Heat until bubbles appear around edge and shortening is melted; cool to lukewarm. Measure water into large bowl and add yeast; stir to dissolve. Add lukewarm milk mixture and eggs. Mix together whole wheat flour, 3 cups white flour, and cinnamon; add to yeast mixture. Beat until smooth. Add raisins and enough flour to make soft dough. Turn out onto floured board; knead until smooth and elastic, kneading in the balance of flour. Put in large greased bowl; turn over, to bring greased side up. Cover; let rise in warm place about 1-1/2 hours, or until the dough doubles in bulk. Punch down; let dough rise about 30 minutes, or until almost doubled in size. Punch down; knead. Divide into 3 parts; place each part in greased bread pan. Cover; let rise 50 to 60 minutes, or until doubled. Bake in 350-degree oven for 30 to 35 minutes.

Banana Fritters

(DENISE KENNARD)

3 bananas
1/2 cup grated pecans
1 cup pastry flour
1-1/2 teaspoons baking powder
1 teaspoon lemon juice

2 tablespoons sugar
1/2 teaspoon salt
1 egg, beaten
1/3 cup milk

Mash bananas; add nuts. Sift flour with baking powder, sugar, and salt; add to bananas and nuts. Add milk, beaten egg, and lemon juice; beat well. Drop by spoonfuls into deep fat; drain on paper. Sprinkle with powdered sugar. Serves 4.

Hush Puppies

(GREG TREMBLE)

1 cup cornmeal
1/4 cup flour
1/4 cup dry egg mix, packed
1/4 teaspoon baking soda
1 teaspoon baking powder
1/2 teaspoon salt
1/2 teaspoon garlic salt
1 small onion, chopped
1 cup buttermilk
fat or oil, 1" deep in fry pan

Stir dry ingredients together until well mixed. Add onion and milk; mix well. Drop batter from teaspoon into hot fat or oil. Fry 2 to 3 minutes until browned on all sides; drain well.

Jalapeno Corn Bread

(KEVIN SMITH)

2-1/2 cups corn meal
1 cup flour
2 tablespoons sugar
1 teaspoon salt
4 teaspoons baking powder
3 eggs, lightly beaten
1-1/2 cups milk
1/2 cup cooking oil
1 can cream-style corn (16 ounces)
2 jalapeno chili peppers, seeded and chopped
2 cups sharp Cheddar cheese, grated
1 onion, grated

In a bowl, combine the first 5 ingredients. Mix the eggs, milk, and oil; add to corn meal mixture. Stir in remaining ingredients; pour into 2 well-greased 11" x 9" baking pans. Bake at 425 degrees for 25 minutes, or until cooked thoroughly.

Buttermilk Biscuits

(KEVIN WILLIAMS)

2 cups flour
1/4 teaspoon baking soda
1/4 cup shortening
1 teaspoon baking powder
1 teaspoon salt
2/3 cup buttermilk

Sift flour with baking powder, baking soda, and salt into a bowl; cut in shortening. Stir in buttermilk. Roll out on floured surface; cut with biscuit cutter. Place on baking sheet. Bake at 450 degrees for 10 minutes.

Corn Bread Stuffing

(KERI MARION)

Prepare 2 boxes "Jiffy" brand corn bread mix, as directed on box. Add 1 cup sugar to batter -- important! Pour the batter into a 13" x 9" x 2" baking dish; bake as directed.

* Prepare corn bread 1 to 2 days ahead of time, and allow to sit uncovered so that bread can thoroughly cool and dry out.

3/4 cup butter
3/4 cut finely-chopped celery, with leaves
1/2 cup chopped green onion
2 cups chopped mushrooms

Heat butter in large Dutch oven. Cook celery, onion, and mushrooms in butter for about 2 minutes. Remove from heat.

Stir in prepared corn bread *(crumbled)*, plus add:

1/2 teaspoon ground sage
1 teaspoon salt
1/4 teaspoon pepper
1/2 teaspoon dried thyme

Mix well until moist and crumbly. Bake at 350 degrees for about 35 to 45 minutes, or until done. Serves 8.

Quick Pizza

(REGGIE BARNES)

1 can Pillsbury Pizza Dough
pizza sauce
meat: sausage/hamburger/pepperoni
onion
green pepper
1 small can black olives
1 small can mushrooms
seasonings: salt/pepper/oregano
cheeses: Mozzarella/Jack/Cheddar cheese

Spread pizza dough on pan. Bake dough for 5 minutes in 400-degree oven. Add pizza sauce. Cook sausage and hamburger meat -- seasoned with salt, pepper, and oregano; drain fat. Add onions and green pepper to meat; simmer. Pour meat on pizza sauce. Add olives and mushrooms. Sprinkle cheeses on top. Bake for 15 minutes. ENJOY!

Scotchy Pull-Aparts

(DAVE CAMPO)

20 Rhodes frozen bread rolls
1/4 cup sugar
1/2 cup melted butter
1 cup brown sugar
1 teaspoon cinnamon
1 package regular butterscotch pudding
pecans

Place frozen rolls in greased and floured Bundt pan. Combine pudding, brown sugar, and cinnamon; sprinkle over rolls. Drizzle butter over the top; sprinkle with nuts. Cover with a kitchen towel; leave overnight. Bake for 30 minutes in 350-degree oven.

Sour Cream Coffee Cake

(DEREK KENNARD)

1/4 pound butter
1 cup sugar
2 eggs
2 cups flour
1 teaspoon baking powder
1 teaspoon baking soda
1/2 teaspoon salt
1 cup sour cream
1 teaspoon vanilla

Cream margarine and sugar until creamy; add eggs.

Add dry ingredients <u>alternately</u> with sour cream. Add vanilla.

Pour half of dough into greased and floured angel food pan. Add half of topping mixture. Add remainder of dough and topping.

Bake at 325 degrees for 45 minutes.

Topping: 1/3 cup brown sugar
1/4 cup white sugar
1-1/4 teaspoons cinnamon
1 cup pecans
1 cup maraschino cherries, cut up

Add ingredients together; mix well.

Monkey Bread

(BILLY DAVIS)

1-1/2 yeast cakes, or 2 packages dry yeast
1 cup milk, heated to lukewarm
4 tablespoons sugar
1 teaspoon salt
1/2 cup melted butter
3-1/2 cups sifted flour

Dissolve yeast in lukewarm milk; stir in sugar, salt, and butter. Add flour; beat well.

Let dough rise to almost double in bulk. Punch down; roll out on lightly-floured board to 1/4" thickness.

Cut in about 2" pieces (round, diamond, or square). Dip each piece in melted butter.

Pile in buttered Bundt pan until half full. Let rise to double in bulk.

Bake at 400 degrees for 30 minutes, or until golden brown.

Serve loaf <u>uncut</u>; let people pull off whatever amount they wish. It is already buttered, so no bread and butter plate is needed.

* This is always a favorite!

Chilled Veggie Pizza

(JOE BRODSKY)

1-1/2 cans Pillsbury Crescent Rolls dough
1 package cream cheese, softened (8 ounces)
1 package dry mix Hidden Valley Ranch Dressing
1 container light sour cream (8 ounces)
fresh broccoli, carrots, red pepper (or vegetables of your
    choice), chopped in processor
1 can sliced black olives
white Cheddar cheese, shredded

Roll out dough on cookie sheet *(don't cut; press down on perforated lines -- flat).* Bake, according to directions on package.

Mix softened cream cheese, sour cream, and Ranch Dressing; spread over cooled crust.

Spread chopped vegetables on top. Then, put sliced olives on top of vegetables.

Spread shredded cheese on top; press down gently. Cool; then cut in squares and serve.

* *May be served warm, but delicious cooled.*

Karen's Yummy Applesauce Walnut Muffins

(KAREN JONES)

1-1/2 cups flour
1 teaspoon baking powder
1 teaspoon baking soda
2 teaspoons cinnamon
1/2 teaspoon salt
3/4 cup oatmeal
2/3 cup brown sugar
1 tablespoon butter, melted
1 egg
2/3 cup applesauce
2/3 cup buttermilk
2/3 cup chopped walnuts

Sift together flour, baking powder, baking soda, cinnamon, and salt. Mix in oatmeal.

Beat egg; add sugar, batter, applesauce, and buttermilk.

Fold wet mixture into dry very gently. Fold in nuts, *but be careful not to over-mix.*

Scoop into greased muffin cups with an ice-cream scooper.

Bake at 375 degrees until lightly browned (about 20 to 25 minutes).

Favorite Waffles

(CONNIE CASE)

3 eggs, separated
1-1/2 cups buttermilk
1 teaspoon baking soda
1-3/4 cups flour
2 teaspoons baking powder
1/2 teaspoon salt
1/2 cup margarine

Add well-beaten egg yolks to buttermilk and baking soda.
Add sifted dry ingredients and melted margarine. Fold in
stiffly-beaten egg whites. Makes 8 to 10 waffles.

** 2 cups sour cream may be used instead of milk and
margarine.*

Cranberry Bread

(RON STONE)

2 cups plain flour
1 cup sugar
1-1/2 teaspoons baking powder
1/2 teaspoon baking soda
1 teaspoon salt
juice and grated rind of 1 orange
2 tablespoons shortening
3/4 cup boiling water
1 egg, beaten
1 cup chopped pecans
1 cup sliced cranberries

(CONTINUED)

Cranberry Bread -- (continued)

Sift the flour and dry ingredients together. Combine orange rind, juice, shortening, and boiling water; blend into the flour mixture. Add egg, pecans, and cranberries; mix well. Pour into greased loaf pan. Bake at 350 degrees for 1 hour. Makes 1 loaf.

Banana-Honey-Nut Muffins

(DAVE LANG)

1-3/4 cups all-purpose flour
2-1/2 teaspoons baking powder
3/4 teaspoon salt
1/3 cup sugar
2/3 cup chopped almonds, toasted
1 egg, beaten
2 tablespoons butter, melted
3/4 cup mashed bananas
1/2 cup, plus 1 tablespoon, milk
1/3 cup vegetable oil
1/4 cup honey
1/3 cup chopped almonds, toasted

In a large bowl, combine first 5 ingredients; make a well in center of mixture. Combine egg, banana, milk, and oil; add to dry mixture, stirring just until moistened. Spoon batter into greased and floured muffin pans, filling 3/4 full. Bake at 400 degrees for 15 minutes, or until golden brown. Remove from pans immediately. Combine honey and butter; mix well. Dip top of muffins in honey mixture, and sprinkle with almonds. Makes 14 muffins.

Mama Pat's Corn Bread Dressing

(GENE JONES)

<u>Corn Bread:</u> Make 2-cup recipe of Aunt Jemima's Corn Meal Mix, as directed on package. Bake, cool, and crumble.

4 to 6 biscuits, or 4 to 6 slices of day-old bread, crumbled
6 soda crackers, crumbled
1 large, or 2 medium yellow onions, diced
2 tablespoons butter
6 celery stalks, with leaves (sliced thin -- 1/4" to 1/2")
2 tablespoons poultry seasoning
salt, to taste
3 cups chicken broth
6 large eggs, beaten

Crumble biscuits, or bread, and crackers. Sauté diced onion in butter.

In a large mixing bowl, mix crumbled bread/cracker mixture, sautéd onions, diced celery, poultry seasoning, and salt together. Add chicken broth and beaten eggs to mixture. Stir sufficiently, making the consistency of thin cake batter; add more broth or milk, if needed.

Pour in 13" x 9" pan. Bake at 350 degrees for 1 hour, or until brown.

Muffin Jewels

(LEON LETT)

1 egg
1 cup milk
1/4 cup salad oil
2 cups sifted all-purpose flour
1/4 cup sugar
3 teaspoons baking powder
1 teaspoon salt
jelly (choose favorite kind)

Preheat oven to 400 degrees. Oil 12 muffin tins, or use paper tin wraps. Beat egg lightly; stir in milk and oil. Sift dry ingredients together; add to mixture. Stir ONLY until the flour is barely moistened *(the batter should be lumpy)*. Fill muffin cups one-half full of batter. Drop a small teaspoonful of jelly in the center. Add more batter to fill muffin tin to 2/3 full. Bake for 20 to 25 minutes.

Crepes

(DIANA BLACKWELL)

2 eggs
2 tablespoons margarine
1-1/4 cups milk
2 tablespoons brandy,
    or orange liqueur

1 tablespoon sugar
1 cup sifted flour
1/2 teaspoon salt

Place ingredients in blender in order listed; blend at high speed for 20 or 30 seconds. Use batter immediately. If thickens, thin with a little milk. If using an electric mixer, pour batter through a sieve for smoothness. Refrigerate for 2 hours before cooking. Makes 16 to 20 crepes.

Mexican Flank Steak

(LARRY ALLEN)

beef flank steak (1 pound)
1/3 cup lime juice
1 teaspoon vegetable oil
1/2 teaspoon salt
1 small onion, chopped (1/4 cup)
2 cloves garlic, finely chopped
1 can chopped green chilies, undrained (4 ounces)

Cut both sides of beef into a diamond pattern 1/8" deep. Place in glass or plastic bowl, or heavy plastic bag.

Mix remaining ingredients; pour over beef, turning beef to coat both sides; cover.

Refrigerate at least 8 hours, but no longer than 24 hours, turning occasionally.

Set oven control to broil. Drain and scrape marinade off beef; reserve marinade.

Place beef on rack in broiler pan. Broil with top 2" to 3" from heat for about 10 minutes (for medium doneness), turning once.

Cut beef across grain at *slanted angle* into thin slices. Heat reserved marinade to boiling; serve over beef.

Italian Stuffed Breast of Veal

(BARRY SWITZER)

breast of veal (4 pounds)
1-1/2 pounds Italian sausage (medium or mild), cooked
  and crumbled
3 cups soft bread crumbs
1/2 cup sliced green onions
1/4 cup chopped Italian parsley
1 egg, slightly beaten
1 teaspoon salt
1/2 teaspoon pepper
1 teaspoon crumbled dried thyme
4 large onions, peeled and sliced
4 carrots, scraped and cut into strips
6 sprigs Italian parsley, chopped
1/2 cup butter
1 cup chicken broth
1/2 cut sauternes

Have butcher cut pocket in veal for stuffing. Combine
sausage with bread crumbs, green onions, 1/4 cup parsley,
egg, salt, pepper, and thyme. Stuff pocket with mixture;
sew up, or fasten with skewers. Mix onions, carrots, and
parsley; spread on the bottom of a large roasting pan.
Dot vegetables with 6 tablespoons of the butter; place
veal on top. Rub veal with remaining butter. Add broth
to roasting pan; sprinkle veal with salt and pepper. Roast
meat at 450 degrees for 30 minutes, *basting 2 or 3 times*.
After 30 minutes, or when slightly browned, pour
sauternes over veal; reduce heat to 325 degrees. Cover
veal and continue roasting for 2-1/2 to 3 hours. Fifteen
minutes before veal is done, remove cover (to finish
browning).

Beef/Tomato with Chinese Noodles

(JOYCE BRODSKY)

1-1/2 pounds top sirloin, sliced very thin in strips
2 stalks celery, sliced diagonally
1 large onion, sliced in circles
1/2 large green pepper, sliced in strips
handful of pea pods
handful of fresh bean sprouts
1 tomato, cut in chunks
2 or 3 fresh green onions, cut up
light soy sauce
1-1/2 tablespoons sugar
2-1/2 tablespoons cornstarch
1 tablespoon beef bouillon
garlic powder
salt and pepper
2 cups water
2-1/2 tablespoons vegetable oil
rice (cooked, according to package directions)
Chinese crispy noodles

Place half of oil in large skillet or wok. Quickly brown strips of beef; add salt, pepper, and garlic powder (a few minutes). Remove beef. Use remainder of oil and <u>quickly</u> stir-fry celery, onions, green peppers; don't overcook. Lower heat. Make paste of cornstarch and about 1/2 cup water. Put remainder of water (1-1/2 cups) into vegetables and beef bouillon; add cornstarch mix to thicken. Heat and keep mixing. When smooth and a nice gravy consistency, add meat, tomatoes, green onions, pea pods, and bean sprouts; mix well. Simmer gently for 5 minutes. Add garlic powder, to taste. Serve over hot rice; add Chinese crispy noodles on top.

Mary's Marinate for Flank Steak or Chicken

(KEVIN O'NEILL)

3 tablespoons sesame seeds
1/4 cup salad oil
1/2 cup soy sauce
2 cloves garlic (can use garlic powder)
1/2 teaspoon black pepper
1/2 teaspoon ginger
1/4 cup brown sugar
2 sliced green onions

Soak overnight; occasionally turning meat.

Shy's Favorite Meatloaf

(SHY ANDERSON)

1-1/2 to 2 pounds lean ground beef
1 can tomato sauce (12 ounces)
3/4 of yellow onion, finely chopped
3/4 tube of saltine crackers, finely crushed
2 eggs
1 tablespoon Worcestershire sauce
1 tablespoon Tiger sauce (optional)
garlic salt
pepper
3 tablespoons ketchup

In large bowl, combine all ingredients above, except for tomato sauce. Add 1/2 can tomato sauce; mix well with your hands. In 13" x 9" casserole, form two loaves. Pour remaining tomato sauce over both loaves. Squirt ketchup down the middle of each loaf, with a dash of Worcestershire sauce. Bake in 350-degree oven for 45 minutes. *Great with mashed potatoes and green beans!*

Beer Steak

(TROY AIKMAN)

1/4 cup butter, or bacon drippings
2 pounds round steak, about 1" thick
flour
1 large onion, chopped
1 cup beer
bouquet garni (1 bay leaf, sprig of parsley, and
    1/4 teaspoon leaf thyme)
salt
freshly-ground pepper

Preheat oven to 275 degrees. Heat butter, in large skillet, over medium-high heat. Dredge meat in flour; brown quickly on both sides. Remove meat; set aside. Add onion to skillet; sauté until softened. Remove half of onions; spread remaining onions evenly in skillet. Place meat on top of onions in skillet; top with reserved onions. Pour in beer; add bouquet garni. Salt and pepper to taste. Cover; bake for 2 hours, or until fork-tender.

Steak Marinate

(CHRIS BONIOL)

1 can of Old Milwaukee Beer (12 ounces)
Italian dressing
Tony Chackerees' Cajun Seasoning
clove of garlic, chopped

Add Italian dressing, cajun seasoning, and clove garlic to beer, as needed, so there is no dominant taste.

* May also be used as a marinate for shrimp and mushrooms.

Spicy Barbecued Brisket

(JACQUE JETT)

1 beef brisket, trimmed of excess fat (4 to 5 pounds)
3 cloves garlic, cut into slivers
2 tablespoons vegetable oil
1 tablespoon coarse, or kosher, salt
1-1/2 teaspoons dried thyme
1 teaspoon freshly-ground pepper
1 teaspoon paprika
1 teaspoon cayenne pepper
basic barbecue sauce (your choice)

Make several slits in the surface of the brisket; poke a sliver of garlic into each one. Rub the brisket with the oil.

In a small bowl, stir together the salt, thyme, pepper, paprika, and cayenne pepper; rub over the meat.

Prepare a fire for indirect-heat cooking in a covered grill. Position the oiled grill rack 4" to 6" above the fire. Place the brisket on the rack -- *not directly over the coals*. Cover the grill; cook for 1 hour, turning once.

Brush with some of the sauce; cook 1 to 1-1/4 hours longer, turning and brushing lightly with sauce two or three times more. Remove from the grill; let rest for 10 minutes.

Carve into thin slices <u>across the grain</u>. Arrange on a warmed platter, and spoon a little sauce over the top.

Wade's Oven-Baked Beef Brisket

(WADE WILSON)

1 well-trimmed boneless brisket (4 to 5 pounds)
liquid smoke
garlic powder
onion powder
celery salt
pepper
Worcestershire sauce
garlic salt

Place brisket in large pan, or casserole dish -- <u>fat side down</u>. Pour liquid smoke over exposed surface of meat, to moisten well. Sprinkle with garlic powder, onion powder, and celery salt. Turn brisket over; repeat on fat side. There should be enough liquid smoke used to cover the bottom of the pan well.

Seal with plastic wrap; refrigerate overnight.

Just before cooking, sprinkle both sides with Worcestershire sauce and garlic salt, ending with fat side up. Seal with foil; bake in 275-degree oven for 4 to 5 hours.

Pour up gravy; chill meat and gravy. Remove fat from gravy. <u>Slice brisket cross-grain</u>. Heat meat and gravy in 350-degree oven when ready to serve.

* For larger brisket: cook 1 hour per pound.

Bar-B-Que Meatballs

(JANE & NEILL ARMSTRONG)

3 pounds ground beef
2 cups quick-cooking oats
2 teaspoons salt
2 teaspoons chili powder
1 teaspoon garlic salt
1 teaspoon pepper
2 eggs
1/2 cup chopped onions
1 large can evaporated milk

Mix all ingredients together; form into medium-size meatballs. Put in a shallow pan. Makes around 50 meatballs, depending on the size.

Sauce:

2 cups ketchup
1/2 cup chopped onion
1 teaspoon garlic salt
2 cups brown sugar (not packed down)
2 tablespoons liquid smoke

Heat all ingredients together in saucepan; stir until boiling. Pour over meatballs. Bake 1 hour in 350-degree oven, uncovered.

* Wonderful do-ahead meat dish -- great for tailgates -- the children love it!

Special Meatballs

(CLAYTON HOLMES)

3 slices bread
1/2 cup milk
1 egg, beaten
1 pound ground beef
3 tablespoons grated onion
1 teaspoon salt
1/8 teaspoon pepper
2 tablespoons shortening
1-1/2 cups tomato juice
1-1/2 cups water
1/2 cup chopped carrots
1/2 cup chopped celery
1/2 teaspoon salt

Soften bread in the milk; add beaten egg. Mix meat, grated onion, 1 teaspoon salt, and pepper. Combine bread and meat mixture. Form into small balls; roll in flour.

In skillet, brown meatballs in hot shortening; drain excess fat. Add tomato juice, water, chopped carrots, chopped celery, and 1/2 teaspoon salt. Cover; simmer for 45 minutes.

Serve with mashed potatoes, or cooked rice. Makes 6 servings.

Cheesed Cutlet

(Godfrey Myles)

1 pound veal cutlet
1/2 teaspoon salt
1/4 teaspoon pepper
1 egg, beaten
2 tablespoons grated Parmesan cheese
1/2 cup fine bread crumbs
1/4 cup salad oil
1 cup sliced onion
1 clove garlic
1/4 cup salad oil
1 can condensed cream of tomato soup, undiluted
1/4 teaspoon dried basil
1/2 teaspoon salt
1/4 teaspoon pepper
1 teaspoon cider vinegar
1/2 cup grated Swiss cheese

Preheat oven to 350 degrees. Cut veal into 4 pieces; pound thin with edge of a saucer. Add salt and pepper to beaten egg. Mix Parmesan cheese with bread crumbs. Dip cutlets in egg; then, in bread crumbs. Heat salad oil in a skillet; sauté cutlets until golden brown. Remove to a shallow baking pan. Using same skillet, sauté onion and garlic in second 1/4 cup salad oil for 5 minutes. Remove garlic. Add remaining ingredients, except for Swiss cheese; simmer for 10 minutes, stirring frequently. Pour over cutlets in the baking pan. Bake at 350 degrees for 35 minutes. Sprinkle grated Swiss cheese over the top; bake for 15 minutes longer. Makes 4 servings.

Mama Minta's BVR BQ Ribs

(JERRY JONES)

6 pounds meaty pork ribs (salt and pepper, to rub)

BVR BQ Sauce:

2 tablespoons cider vinegar
2 teaspoons dry mustard
3 tablespoons Worcestershire sauce
1/2 cup soy sauce
small frozen orange juice *(do not dilute)*
1/4 cup light brown sugar
1/4 teaspoon cayenne pepper
4 teaspoons lemon juice
3/4 cup honey *(do not dilute)*

Have butcher cut ribs in approximately 3" pieces. Line pan (16" x 12" x 2-1/2") with aluminum foil.

Pour 1 cup water into pan; place rubbed ribs onto rack in pan. Cover pan completely with foil. Bake for 1 hour at 350 degrees.

While ribs are cooking, heat sauce ingredients, in small pan, to a boil. After 1 hour, remove foil from top of rib pan; leave in oven for another 30 minutes, basting 4 times with "BVR BQ Sauce" *(until glazed)*.

Remove from pan. Serve . . . and ENJOY!

Pork and Shrimp Chow Mein

(JULI WOODSON)

1/2 pound Chinese noodles
2 tablespoons peanut oil
1/2 pound pork fillet, sliced
1 carrot, shredded
1 red pepper, thinly sliced
bean sprouts (3 ounces)
snow pea pods (2 ounces)
1 tablespoon rice wine, or dry sherry
2 tablespoons soy sauce
1/4 pound cooked, peeled shrimp

Cook the noodles in boiling salted water for about 5 minutes. Rinse under hot water; drain well. Heat oil in wok; stir-fry pork (for 5 minutes) until almost cooked. Add carrots; cook for 1 minute. Add red pepper, bean sprouts, snow pea pods, wine or sherry, and soy sauce; cook for 2 minutes. Add noodles and shrimp; toss over lightly. Heat for 2 minutes. Serve immediately.

Easy Pork Chops and Rice

(SCOTT CASE)

1-1/4 cups instant rice
1/2 envelope dry onion soup mix
1 can cream of mushroom, or celery, soup (10-3/4 ounces)
1-1/4 cups boiling water
1/4 cup Rose wine (optional)
6 pork chops
salt and pepper, to taste

Combine rice, soup mix, soup, water, and wine in a buttered 13" x 9" casserole. Brown the chops; season with salt and pepper. Place on top of rice; bake, covered, at 350 degrees for 1 hour and 15 minutes. Serves 6.

Ham Loaf with Hot Mustard Sauce

(MICHAEL BATISTE)

2 pounds ground ham
2 pounds lean ground pork
2 eggs, beaten
1-1/2 cups bread crumbs (toast bread and grind fine)
1 can tomato soup
2 soup cans water

Hot Mustard Sauce:

1/4 cup dry mustard
1/4 cup white wine tarragon vinegar
2 tablespoons sugar
1/8 teaspoon salt
1 egg
1/2 cup Hellman's mayonnaise

Combine all the loaf ingredients; divide in half. Place in two lightly-greased loaf pans. Place the pans in a large shallow pan containing 1/2" water.

Bake the loaves at 275 degrees for 3 hours.

Prepare the sauce while the loaves are baking. In a saucepan, combine all the ingredients, except the mayonnaise. Cook over low heat until mixture is thickened -- stirring <u>constantly</u>.

Refrigerate until cooled; stir in the mayonnaise.

Sweet and Sour Pork

(HURVIN MCCORMACK)

1 pound lean pork
salt and pepper, to taste
1 teaspoon soy sauce
vegetable oil
flour
1 cup carrots, finely chopped
1/2 cup diced green bell peppers

Cut 1 pound lean pork into pieces about 1/4" thick, 1/2" wide, and 1" long; add salt and pepper, to taste, and soy sauce. Fry pieces of pork in vegetable oil. When well done, roll pork in flour; broil for 5 minutes in <u>very hot (boiling)</u> oil. Remove the pork; broil the carrots and bell peppers for 1 minute in the oil. Mix the pork, carrots, and bell peppers together; serve with hot "Sweet and Sour Sauce". Makes 6 servings.

Sweet and Sour Sauce:

1 cup sugar
3/4 cup white vinegar
1 teaspoon salt
1 teaspoon soy sauce
1 teaspoon lemon juice
1 teaspoon catsup
1 teaspoon garlic, finely chopped

Mix sauce ingredients together well.

Greek-Style Baked Chicken

(TAMMY HENNINGS)

4 chicken breast halves (boneless, skinless)
1 Roma tomato, finely diced
2 tablespoons chopped, fresh parsley
1 tablespoon chopped, fresh mint
1/4 teaspoon dried oregano
freshly-grated black pepper (doesn't have to be fresh)
2 tablespoons diced yellow, or red, bell peppers
4 tablespoons Feta cheese, crumbled
1 teaspoon extra-virgin olive oil

Preheat oven to 375 degrees. Lightly coat baking dish with cooking spray.

Arrange chicken in dish; set aside.

In bowl, combine tomato, parsley, mint, oregano, black pepper, and Feta cheese; mix well. Spoon over each breast. Drizzle olive oil over all.

Bake for 25 minutes, or until chicken is firm.

Serve with cooked rice, angel hair pasta, or with onion-roasted potatoes *(recipe on page 369).*

VERY TASTY AND LIGHT!

Pineapple Chicken

(JANICE FORD)

8 chicken breast halves (skinless, boneless)
1 cup Catalina Salad Dressing
1/2 cup pineapple preserves
1 envelope dry onion soup mix

In a bowl, combine dressing, preserves, and soup mix. Place chicken in 13" x 9" baking pan; top chicken with dressing mixture. Cover with foil; bake at 350 degrees for 20 minutes --baste. Bake, uncovered, 25 minutes longer, or until juices are clear. Serve over, or with, rice or buttered pasta.

Italiano Chicken for Four

(OSCAR STURGIS)

1/2 cup shredded Parmesan cheese
2 teaspoons minced parsley
1 teaspoon oregano leaves
1/4 teaspoon crushed, fresh garlic
dash of black pepper
2 chicken breasts, split (boneless and skinless)
3 tablespoons butter
rice or pasta (cooked, according to package directions)

Mix the cheese, oregano, parsley, and pepper together well. Dip chicken in melted butter; then, into mixture, <u>coating well</u>. Put in a large baking dish; drizzle any remaining butter over chicken breasts. Bake in preheated, 375-degree oven for 25 minutes until chicken is done. Serve over rice or pasta . . . then, EAT!

Italian Chicken Cutlets

(BARRY SWITZER)

6 chicken breast halves, skinless and boneless
1 cup Italian-seasoned bread crumbs
1/2 cup freshly-grated Romano, or Parmesan, cheese
1/4 cup all-purpose flour
1 envelope light Italian salad dressing mix (0.8 ounces)
2 teaspoons dried whole oregano
1/4 teaspoon garlic powder
2 eggs, beaten
1/3 cup vegetable oil
green onion strips (optional)

Place each piece of chicken between 2 sheets of wax paper; flatten to 1/4" thickness, using a meat mallet or rolling pin.

Combine bread crumbs and next 5 ingredients. Dip chicken in eggs; dredge in bread-crumb mixture.

In a large skillet, heat vegetable oil over medium heat. Add chicken; cook 3 to 4 minutes on each side, or until golden brown (adding extra oil, if necessary). Drain on paper towels.

Garnish with green onion strips, if desired. Makes 6 servings.

Grilled Turkey Drumsticks

(GREG TREMBLE)

4 turkey drumsticks
1/3 cup vegetable oil
1/3 cup dry sherry
1/4 cup chopped, fresh parsley
1/4 cup butter, melted
1/3 cup soy sauce
1 clove garlic, minced
1/4 teaspoon salt
1/4 teaspoon pepper
1/4 cup chopped onion

Place turkey drumsticks in a large shallow dish. Combine remaining ingredients, stirring well. Pour over drumsticks; cover.

Marinate in refrigerator 8 hours, turning drumsticks occasionally.

Drain drumsticks, <u>reserving marinade</u>. Wrap each drumstick and 1/4 cup marinade in heavy-duty aluminum foil. Grill over medium coals for 1 hour, turning after 30 minutes.

Remove foil, <u>reserving marinade</u>. Return drumsticks to grill; continue cooking 30 to 40 minutes, basting <u>frequently</u> with reserved marinade. Makes 8 servings.

The Blake's Un-Fried Chicken

(JOHN BLAKE)

The secret to the success of this recipe is to make sure that both the chicken and the yogurt are *very cold* (perhaps soaking the chicken in ice water). The preliminary soaking will help the breading adhere and produce a crisp coating much like that of fried chicken.

light vegetable oil cooking spray
6 chicken drumsticks, skin removed
3 whole chicken breasts, halved and skinless
3-1/2 cups ice water
1 cup plain non-fat yogurt

Breading:

1 cup dried Italian bread crumbs
1 cup all-purpose flour
1 tablespoon Oki Bay seasoning
1/2 teaspoon garlic powder
1/2 teaspoon Creole seasoning
1/8 teaspoon freshly-ground black pepper
dash of cayenne pepper
1/2 teaspoon dried thyme
1/2 teaspoon dried basil
1/2 teaspoon dried oregano

Preheat oven to 400 degrees. Coat a baking sheet with 3 sprays of vegetable oil. In a large bowl, put chicken with the ice water. Put yogurt into a medium bowl. Set both bowls aside.

(CONTINUED)

The Blake's Un-Fried Chicken -- (continued)

Toss all breading ingredients into a large, tightly-sealing plastic bag. Seal; shake well to mix. Remove 2 pieces of chicken from ice water; roll each piece in yogurt. Put chicken into the plastic bag; reseal, and shake to coat thoroughly. Transfer breaded chicken to prepared baking sheet. Repeat process, until all 12 pieces are breaded. Spray chicken lightly with the vegetable oil. Place baking sheet on the bottom shelf of the oven; bake for 1 hour, turning the pieces every 20 minutes to allow even browning. Serve hot, or at room temperature.

Logan's Lemon Pepper Chicken

(CRISS LACEWELL)

chicken breasts (as many as desired)
lemon juice
lemon pepper
Jane's Crazy Salt
pasta, rice, or potatoes (whichever desired)

Line a glass or ceramic baking dish with aluminum foil. Place desired number of chicken breasts in baking dish *(be sure to leave the skin on and bone in -- helps make juice thicken).* Pour in lemon juice to cover 1/2" to 3/4" bottom of pan. Season with a lot of Jane's Crazy Salt and, also, lots of lemon pepper. Cook, uncovered, at 450 degrees for approximately 45 minutes. Chicken should get brown and crispy, and sauce thickened and bubbly.

* This sauce is great on pasta, rice, or potatoes.

Stir-Fried Lemon Chicken

(CHARLES HALEY)

2 lemons
2 teaspoons cornstarch
1 teaspoon sugar
1/2 cup chicken broth
2 tablespoons dry sherry
2 tablespoons soy sauce
1/4 cup vegetable oil
2 whole chicken breasts (skinless and boneless), cut into
    1/4" pieces
salt and pepper, to taste
1/2 cup thinly-sliced carrots
1/4 cup water chestnuts, cut into strips
1/4 cup pea pods, cut into strips
4 green onions, cut into 1/2" pieces
1/2 medium red bell pepper, cut into strips

Cut 1/8" strips of lemon peel from 1/2 of 1 lemon; set aside. Slice other half; reserve for garnish. Squeeze juice from second lemon. Combine cornstarch and sugar in small bowl. Add 2 tablespoons lemon juice, chicken broth, sherry, and soy sauce; blend well. Set aside. Heat wok, or large skillet, over medium-high heat, until hot. Add oil; *heat until it ripples.* Sprinkle chicken with salt and pepper. Stir-fry for 3 minutes, or until chicken is done. Remove chicken to serving platter; keep warm. Add carrots, water chestnuts, pea pods, onions, and red peppers to wok. Stir-fry for 1 minute. Add lemon juice mixture to vegetables; stir-fry for 1 minute, or until thickened. Return chicken to skillet; add lemon strips and stir-fry for 1 minute. Makes 4 servings.

* Serve with hot cooked rice. Garnish with lemon slices.

Chicken Enchilada Bake

(JIM EDDY)

2 tablespoons butter, or margarine
1/2 cup chopped onion
1 garlic clove, minced
1/2 cup sliced, ripe olives
1 can diced green chilies, drained (4 ounces)
1/4 cup milk
1/2 cup dairy sour cream
1 can condensed cream of chicken soup (10-1/2 ounces)
1-1/2 cup cubed, cooked chicken
1 cup shredded Cheddar cheese (4 ounces)
8 flour, or corn, tortillas

Preheat oven to 350 degrees.

In medium saucepan, melt butter; sauté onion and garlic in butter until tender. Stir in 1/4 cup of the ripe olives, green chilies, sour cream, and soup; mix well. Reserve 3/4 cup sauce; set aside. Fold in chicken and 1/2 cup of the cheese to remaining sauce.

Warm tortillas, as directed on package. Fill tortillas with chicken mixture; roll up. Place seam side down in ungreased 12" x 8" baking dish (2-quart).

In small bowl, combine reserved 3/4 cup sauce and milk; spoon over tortillas. Bake at 350 degrees for 30 to 35 minutes, or until bubbly. To serve, sprinkle with remaining cheese and olives. Makes 8 enchiladas.

Charlotte's Rotel Chicken

(CHARLOTTE JONES ANDERSON)

1 pound Lite Velveeta cheese, cubed
6 chicken breasts
1 tablespoon tarragon
1 tablespoon oregano
olive oil
1 onion, chopped
1 bell pepper, chopped (optional)
fresh mushrooms
garlic salt
1 can Rotel diced tomatoes with chilies
spaghetti, or linguini (8-ounce package)

Boil chicken in salted water with 1 tablespoon tarragon and 1 tablespoon oregano (*best flavor -- if breast has skin and bone*). Cook; cut into bite-sized pieces. Save broth to cook spaghetti.

Sauté onion and bell pepper in olive oil. Add mushrooms, and sprinkle garlic salt while sautéing. Add Rotel tomatoes and Velveeta cheese. Cook until the cheese melts.

Put all of the ingredients in a casserole (3-quart). Bake at 350 degrees for 45 minutes, uncovered. Serves 6.

Chicken Wellington with Champagne Sauce

(BRENDA SCHWANTZ)

6 chicken breasts, boneless and skinless
6 tablespoons butter, divided
salt and white pepper, to taste
2 packages of frozen puff pastry
6 thin slices of ham
6 thin slices of Mozzarella cheese
2 eggs, lightly beaten

Champagne Sauce (optional):

1 pound mushrooms, sliced
2 tablespoons butter, if needed
4 to 5 cups half and half, warmed
1/8 teaspoon salt
1/8 teaspoon white pepper
1/8 teaspoon thyme
1/4 cup flour
1 cup of champagne, at room temperature
minced parsley

Sauté chicken breasts in 3 tablespoons butter until lightly browned on each side; season with salt and pepper. Remove with slotted spoon; save pan and remaining butter. Open breast; place 1 slice of ham and 1 slice of cheese in the breast. Roll dough to twice the size of each breast.

(CONTINUED)

Chicken Wellington with Champagne Sauce
(continued)

Place 1 breast <u>diagonally</u> in center of each square. Fold 1 corner of dough square to center. Brush top of corner with egg. Fold in each corner, brushing tops.

With a cookie cutter, cut decorative designs from scraps of dough. Brush top of dough "envelope" with egg; stick cut out to top.

Place chicken in large, shallow baking pan; brush tops with egg. Bake in preheated 350-degree oven for 45 to 60 minutes, or until golden brown.

While chicken bakes, sauté mushrooms for 5 minutes in reserved pan with butter. Remove with slotted spoon. Add enough butter to pan to equal 4 tablespoons. Blend in flour. Stir over high heat for 2 minutes, making sure roux does not brown. Add salt, pepper and thyme. Reduce heat; add cream slowly until thoroughly blended. *Do not boil.* Stir in champagne; add mushrooms. Simmer for 15 minutes, or until sauce is reduced by one-third. Taste . . . and correct seasoning.

Pour into sauce boat. Sprinkle with parsley. Serve <u>immediately</u> with chicken.

Glazed Citrus Chicken

(KAREN HALEY)

2 large whole chicken breasts, halved (skinless)
2 oranges, cut in halves
2 lemons, cut in halves
2 limes, cut in halves
1 tablespoon seasoned salt
1 tablespoon seasoned pepper
1 can apricot halves, drained (12 ounces)
2 tablespoons brown sugar
1 tablespoon margarine, or butter
dash of nutmeg
mint leaves

Place chicken in glass baking dish. Squeeze juice from one-half of each orange, lemon, and lime over the chicken. Thinly slice remaining citrus fruit; set aside for garnish.

Sprinkle seasoning salt and seasoning pepper evenly over chicken. Cover; bake in 400-degree oven for 30 minutes.

While chicken is baking, prepare glaze. Pureé apricot halves in blender. In small saucepan, combine the apricot puree, brown sugar, butter, and nutmeg. Heat until bubbles appear. Reduce heat; cover. Simmer for 5 minutes, stirring occasionally. Pour glaze over chicken breasts.

Bake, uncovered, for 10 minutes longer. Garnish with mint, if desired. Makes 4 servings.

Chef Marky's Favorite Kobe-Style Fish

(MARK TUINEI)

3 good-size fillets of white fish, sea bass, or halibut
1 bunch cilantro (separate leaves, and cut stems)
1 large piece of fresh ginger, sliced
3 different oils: 1/2 cup peanut oil
                      1/4 cup olive
                      1/4 cup sesame
soy sauce *

In a large pot, combine cilantro stems, fresh ginger slices, and enough water to cover three fish fillets. Bring water to boil; add fillets. Boil carefully until cooked *(fillet should be white and flake with an easy touch with a fork)*. Drain; discard ginger and cilantro stems.

Place fillet on serving platter *(heat resistant)*. Beat three different oils simultaneously, so to sear fish with oil combination when placed onto serving place: use oils . . . make sure to cover all of fillets. Top with cilantro leaves and soy sauce, to taste. <u>Caution</u>: *may be salty if too much is added.*

Serve with steamed white or brown rice. Serves three people.

* Our choice is "Aloha Shoyu" -- found at Kazy's Gourmet Shop in Dallas, or anywhere in Hawaii.

Vikki's Shrimp Scampi

(VIKKI ZIMMER)

1-1/4 pounds medium shrimp, shelled and deveined
4 tablespoons diet margarine, melted
2 large, or 4 small, garlic cloves, crushed
1/2 teaspoon salt
1/2 teaspoon pepper
paprika
parsley springs *(for garnish)*

Preheat broiler. In shallow, 2-quart, flameproof casserole, arrange shrimp. In small bowl, combine remaining ingredients, except parsley; pour mixture over shrimp. Toss to coat. Broil 3" to 4" from heat source, until shrimp are golden brown (about 1 to 2 minutes). Garnish with parsley. Makes 4 servings.

* Calories - 178 per serving; saturated fat - less than 1 gram

Cheesy Trout Fillets

(TRACEY FLEMING)

46 butterflied trout fillets
1 medium onion, chopped
2 tablespoons butter, melted
1 can cream of shrimp soup, undiluted
1/2 cup half and half
1/2 cup Swiss cheese, finely-shredded
1/2 cup Cheddar cheese, finely-shredded
paprika

Preheat oven to 325 degrees. Place thawed trout fillets in shallow, lightly-oiled baking dish. In saucepan, saute onions in butter until tender. Stir in next 4 ingredients; stir carefully until cheese melts. Spoon mixture over trout fillets; sprinkle with paprika. Bake for 20 minutes. Serves 4 to 6 people.

Stuffed Sole

(STEVE HOFFMAN)

1 cup chopped onion
2 cans shrimp, rinsed and drained (4-1/4 ounces each)
1 jar sliced mushrooms, drained (4-1/2 ounces)
2 tablespoons butter, or margarine
1/2 pound fresh, cooked (or canned) crab meat, drained --
  with cartilage removed
8 sole, or flounder fillets (2 to 2-1/2 pounds)
1/2 teaspoon salt
1/4 teaspoon pepper
1/4 teaspoon paprika
2 cans condensed cream of mushroom soup, undiluted
  (10-3/4 ounces each)
1/3 cup chicken broth
2 tablespoons water
2/3 cup shredded Cheddar cheese
2 tablespoons minced, fresh parsley
cooked wild, brown, or white rice, or a mixture *(optional)*

In a saucepan, saute onion, shrimp, and mushrooms in
butter until onion is tender. Add crab meat; heat through.

Sprinkle fillets with salt, pepper, and paprika. Spoon crab
meat mixture on fillets; roll up and fasten with a toothpick.

Place in a greased 13" x 9" x 2" baking dish. Combine the
soup, broth, and water; blend until smooth. Pour over
fillets. Sprinkle with cheese. Cover; bake at 400 degrees
for 30 minutes.

Sprinkle with parsley. Return to the oven, uncovered, for
5 minutes, or until the fish flakes easily with a fork. Serve
over rice, if desired. Makes 8 servings.

Shrimp Creole

(MARY SMITH, MOTHER OF EMMITT SMITH)

1-1/2 pounds cleaned, peeled, and deveined shrimp
1 cup onions, chopped
1/2 cup green bell pepper, chopped
4 cloves garlic pods, minced
1/2 cup oil, or 1/4 pound margarine
1 can tomato sauce (6 ounces)
1 can tomato paste (6 ounces)
1 teaspoon sugar
1 cup green onion tops and parsley
1 cup celery, chopped
3 cups water
salt, to taste
black pepper, to taste
cayenne, to taste
rice (cooked, according to package directions)

Clean shrimp; season with salt, black pepper, and cayenne. Set this aside.

Heat oil, or margarine, in Dutch oven over medium heat; cook onions and celery until onions are wilted.

Add tomato paste; fry another 5 minutes, stirring constantly. Add tomato sauce and 2 cups of water; cook about 40 minutes, or until oil comes to the top. Stir occasionally. If sauce gets too thick, add a little more water. Add shrimp, green bell pepper, garlic, sugar, salt, black pepper, and cayenne. Cook for 30 minutes, or until shrimp are tender. Serve over cooked rice.

OUTSTANDING!

Elsie's Baked Fish

(ELSIE HOUCK)

3 tablespoons melted butter
1 onion, thinly sliced
1-1/2 pounds red snapper, or orange roughy
1/2 cup mayonnaise
1/4 cup Parmesan cheese
2 tablespoons lemon juice
1 teaspoon Worcestershire sauce
1/2 teaspoon paprika
1/2 teaspoon salt
oregano
chopped parsley

Pour butter on bottom of 13" x 9" baking dish. Arrange onion evenly on bottom of dish. Place single layer of fish on top of onion.

Combine mayonnaise, cheese, lemon juice, Worcestershire sauce, paprika, and salt together; spread evenly over fish. Sprinkle oregano and parsley on top.

Bake at 350 degrees for 35 to 40 minutes.

Quick-Fried Shrimp

(DARREN WOODSON)

2 pounds cooked shrimp
2 cloves garlic, crushed
1" piece fresh ginger, finely-chopped
1 tablespoon chopped, fresh coriander
3 tablespoons peanut oil
1 tablespoon dry sherry
2 tablespoons light soy sauce
4 green onions, sliced
rice (cooked, according to package directions)

Shell the shrimp, <u>leaving on the tails</u>. Place shrimp in a bowl with all the remaining ingredients, except the green onions; let marinate for 30 minutes. Heat a wok; add the shrimp and marinade. Stir-fry for 10 minutes, or until heated through. Serve sprinkled with sliced green onions over steamed white rice.

Crisp Fried Catfish

(KENDELL WATKINS)

6 medium catfish, cleaned and dressed
1 teaspoon salt
1/4 teaspoon pepper
1 bottle hot sauce (2 ounces)
2 cups self-rising cornmeal
vegetable oil
fresh parsley springs *(optional)*

(CONTINUED)

Crisp Fried Catfish -- (continued)

Sprinkle catfish with salt and pepper. Marinate in hot sauce for 1 to 2 hours in the refrigerator. Place cornmeal in a paper bag; drop in catfish (<u>one at a time</u>) and shake until completely coated. Fry -- in deep hot oil over high heat until fish float to the top and are golden brown; drain well. Serve hot. Garnish with parsley, if desired. Makes 6 servings.

Marinated Frogs' Legs

(EDWARD HERVEY)

1/2 cup cider vinegar
1 bay leaf, crumbled
1 tablespoon chopped parsley
1 small onion, minced
4 pair frogs' legs
flour
1/4 cup butter
salt, to taste

Combine first 4 ingredients in a shallow dish. Place frogs' legs in vinegar mixture; marinate overnight in the refrigerator. Spoon marinade over frogs' legs several times.

Drain; wipe dry. Roll in flour; saute in butter over low heat until brown on both sides. Season with salt; serve hot. Makes 4 servings.

Seafood Stock
(including shrimp, crawfish, and fish stocks)

(ROBERT BLACKWELL)

1 medium onion, peeled and quartered
3 stalks celery, coarsely cut
1 whole clove garlic, peeled

This mixture should just cover a variety of good seafood stock makers, such as fresh shrimp heads and/or shells, or lobster heads and/or shells, any fresh fish bones, oyster liquor, or any combination of these. If shrimp, crawfish, or fish stock is called for, use the shells, bones, etc., of the particular fish specified.

Bring the ingredients to a rapid boil; then, reduce heat to a slow simmer. Cook at least 2 hours, no more than 8.

When making a stock, the best flavors are achieved by making the stock as clear as possible.

After stock is cooked, strain it; then, reduce it for additional flavor. *(If you have a sauce that calls for a small amount of liquid or stock but needs a lot of taste, reduction is necessary.)*

Take stock and pour into a skillet or pot. Simmer, uncovered, until evaporation reduces it to half its original quantity. For instance, 1 quart of good stock can be reduced to 1 cup or less by slow evaporation. In some instances, 1 or 2 tablespoons of reduced stock make the difference between a mediocre and a fantastic dish.

Abby Lambert's Crawfish Pistolettes

(COUSIN OF CHRIS BONIOL)

1 onion, chopped
1 bell pepper, chopped
2 ribs celery, chopped
1 clove garlic, chopped
1 stick of butter
2 pounds crawfish tails
1 can mushroom pieces
Tony Chachere's Creole Seasoning, to taste
1 can cream of mushroom soup
3 tablespoons chopped parsley
30 pistolettes

Sauté vegetables in butter. Add crawfish, mushrooms, and seasoning; cook for 15 minutes. Add mushroom soup and parsley; simmer for 5 minutes on low heat. Let cool.

Cut off tip of pistolette. Remove some of the bread from the inside; replace with crawfish mixture. Replace bread tip. Spread melted butter and garlic powder on top of pistolette.

Bake at 450 degrees for 8 minutes. Makes 30 pistolettes. <u>Freezes well</u>.

* *Calories per serving: 293 calories (2 pistolettes)*

Bucky's Shrimp Gumbo

(Bᴜᴄᴋʏ Bᴜᴄʜᴀɴᴀɴ)

2 cups sliced, fresh okra, or 10-ounce package frozen
   okra, sliced
1/3 cup shortening, melted
1/3 cup chopped green onions, and tops
3 cloves garlic, finely chopped
1-1/2 teaspoons salt
1/2 teaspoon pepper
1-pound package fully-peeled, deveined shrimp (raw
   or frozen)
2 cups hot water
1 cup canned tomatoes
2 whole bay leaves
6 drops hot pepper sauce
1-1/2 cups cooked rice

Sauté okra in shortening about 10 minutes, or until okra appears dry; stir constantly. Add onion, garlic, salt, pepper, and shrimp; cook about 5 minutes. Add water, tomatoes, and bay leaves. Cover; simmer for 20 minutes.

Remove bay leaves. Add hot pepper sauce.

Place 1/4 cup rice in bottom of each of 6 soup bowls; fill with gumbo. Makes 6 servings.

Bruce's Jambalaya

(BRUCE MAYS)

1/2 cup Canola oil
1/4 cup flour
1 onion, chopped
1/2 green pepper, chopped
2 stalks celery, chopped
1-1/4 pound lean ground beef
1/4 teaspoon pepper
1 teaspoon salt
1 package Lipton Dry Onion Soup
2 cups water
1 pound raw shrimp, shelled
2 cups long-grain rice, uncooked

Make roux by browning flour in oil until dark brown -- don't let it burn. Add onion, green pepper, and celery to roux; sauté for about 4 minutes.

Add lean ground beef to roux; cook until browned. Drain off fat. Add 2 cups water and Lipton Dry Onion Soup; cover.

After Jambalaya has been salted and peppered to taste, simmer for 10 minutes. Add shrimp; simmer 5 minutes, covered. Add cooked rice to Jambalaya. Serve.

Hint: Prepare long-grain rice by soaking for 30 minutes in water. Drain rice; add to 3 cups boiling water. Simmer, covered, for 20 minutes.

Baked Red Snapper

(RON STONE)

8 red snapper fillets
paprika
salad oil

Sauce: 1 quart water
2 tablespoons cornstarch
1/2 stick butter
1/2 cup lemon juice

Season fish with salt and pepper; place in a lightly-greased, shallow baking dish. Sprinkle with paprika and small amount of oil. Put in pre-heated 400-degree oven; brown. In saucepan, heat water; add remaining ingredients. Beat with wire whisk until mixture is slightly thickened; pour over fish. Reduce heat to 350 degrees; bake for 30 minutes.

Bass Fillets

(LEON LETT)

4 bass fillets
1 can shrimp soup (10-3/4 ounces)
1 tablespoon minced onion
2 teaspoons Worcestershire sauce
1/4 cup grated cheese and bread crumbs

Bake fillets (plain) in 350-degree oven for 7 to 8 minutes in lightly-greased, glass baking dish. Mix shrimp soup, minced onion, and Worcestershire sauce together; cover fish with mixture. Sprinkle with cheese and bread crumbs. Broil (for 2 or 3 minutes) until crumbs brown. Serves 4.

Cajun Catfish Skillet

(HUBBARD "AXE" ALEXANDER)

2 cups water
1 cup uncooked rice *
1/4 teaspoon salt
1/4 teaspoon ground red pepper
1/4 teaspoon ground white pepper
1/4 teaspoon ground black pepper
1/2 cup minced green onions
1/2 cup minced green pepper
1/2 cup minced celery
2 cloves garlic, minced
1 tablespoon margarine
1 pound catfish nuggets, or other firm-flesh white fish **
1 can tomato sauce (15-1/2 ounces)
1 teaspoon dried oregano leaves

In 3-quart saucepan, combine water, rice, salt, red pepper, white pepper, and black pepper. Bring to a boil; stir. Reduce heat; cover, and simmer 15 minutes, or until rice is tender and liquid is absorbed. In large skillet, cook onions, green pepper, celery, and garlic in margarine (over medium-high heat) until tender.

Stir vegetable mixture, catfish nuggets, tomato sauce, and oregano into hot rice. Cover; cook over medium heat for 7 to 8 minutes, or until catfish flakes with fork. Makes 4 servings.

 * Recipe based on regular long-grain white rice
** Substitute one pound of chicken nuggets for fish, if desired.

Spicy Cajun Shrimp

(CORY FLEMING)

1 pound jumbo shrimp, finely chopped
1/4 cup flour
1/2 cup butter
1 cup onion, chopped
1/2 cup green pepper, chopped
1/2 cup celery, chopped
1 large clove of garlic, minced
1/4 teaspoon lemon juice
1 cup water
rice (cooked, according to package directions)

Thaw shrimp and chop.

In large saucepan, combine flour and butter; cook over medium heat, stirring until turns golden (about 15 to 20 minutes).

Add onion, green pepper, celery, and garlic; saute for 20 minutes. Add shrimp and remaining ingredients. Bring to boil; then, simmer for 3 to 5 minutes, or until shrimp is tender. Season.

Serve over a bed of rice. Makes 4 to 6 servings.

Onion-Roasted Potatoes

(Chad Hennings)

1 envelope Lipton Recipe Secrets Onion Soup Mix
2 pounds potatoes, cut into large chunks
1/3 extra-virgin olive oil

Preheat oven to 450 degrees. In large zip-lock bag, combine all ingredients. Close bag; shake until evenly coated. Empty potatoes into shallow baking pan. Bake for 40 minutes, stirring occasionally. Top with parsley.

Fried Green Tomato Slices

(George Hegamin)

4 green tomatoes, thickly sliced
2 eggs, beaten
1/2 cup yellow corn meal
1/4 teaspoon salt
black pepper
1/3 cup shortening

Wash tomatoes; remove stem ends. Cut each tomato in 3 or 4 thick slices crosswise. Dip tomato slices in the beaten eggs. Combine corn meal, salt, and pepper; dip egg-coated tomatoes in mixture. In a heavy skillet, heat shortening; sauté tomato slices quickly until brown on both sides. Makes 4 servings.

Raffy's Asparagus Cheese Strata

(RAFFY HOFFMAN)

1-1/2 pounds fresh asparagus, cut into 2" pieces
3 tablespoons butter, or margarine, melted
1-pound loaf sliced bread, crusts removed
3/4 cup shredded Cheddar cheese, divided
2 cups cubed ham, fully cooked
6 eggs
3 cups milk
2 teaspoons dried minced onion
1/2 teaspoon salt
1/4 teaspoon dry mustard

In a saucepan, cover asparagus with water; cover. Cook until just tender but still firm. Drain; set aside.

Lightly brush butter over one side of bread slices. Place half of bread, *buttered side up*, in greased 13" x 9" x 2" baking dish. Sprinkle with 1/2 cup cheese. Layer with asparagus and ham. Cover with remaining bread, *buttered side up.*

In a bowl, lightly beat eggs; add milk, onion, salt, and mustard. Pour over bread. Cover; refrigerate overnight. Bake, uncovered, at 325 degrees for 50 minutes. Sprinkle with remaining cheese. Return to the oven for 10 minutes, or until cheese is melted and a knife inserted near the center comes out clean. Makes 10 to 12 servings.

Bates' Tennessee Corn *

(BILL BATES)

1 can corn, drained (#10 can)
1 can hominy, drained ((#10 can)
1 pound butter
1 quart sour cream
2-1/2 pounds pepper Jack cheese, grated

Mix all ingredients; pour into a six-inch half pan. Bake at 350 degrees for 30 minutes. Serves several people.

* *Served at Bill Bates' new restaurant,* "BILL BATES COWBOY GRILL."

Robert's Zucchini Patties

(ROBERT BLACKWELL)

3 cups grated zucchini
1 small onion, minced
1 small carrot, grated
3/4 cup all-purpose flour
3/4 teaspoon baking powder
1 extra-large egg, lightly beaten
1/2 teaspoon salt
1/4 teaspoon white pepper
3 tablespoons butter
3 tablespoons vegetable oil

Combine all ingredients, except butter and oil, in large mixing bowl; mix well. Heat butter and oil in large skillet. Shape zucchini mixture into patties. Fry until golden brown on each side. Makes 8 to 10 servings.

Buttercrust Corn Pie

(KEVIN O'NEILL)

1-1/4 cups finely-crushed saltine crackers
1/4 cup grated Parmesan cheese
1/2 cup butter, or margarine, melted
1-1/4 cups milk, divided
2 cups fresh, or frozen, corn
1/2 to 1 teaspoon onion salt
1/4 teaspoon ground white pepper
2 tablespoons all-purpose flour
1/4 cup chopped ripe olives
1/2 cup sliced green onions
2 large eggs, lightly-beaten
paprika
fresh tomato salsa

Combine first 3 ingredients, stirring well; reserve 2 tablespoons. Press remaining cracker mixture into bottom and up sides of a 9" pie plate; set aside. In a saucepan, combine 1 cup milk, corn, salt, pepper, and, if desired, sugar; bring to a boil over medium heat. Reduce heat; simmer mixture for 3 minutes. Combine remaining 1/4 cup milk and flour; stir until smooth. Gradually add flour mixture to corn mixture, stirring constantly (mixture will be thick). Remove from heat. Stir in olives and onions. Gradually stir about one-fourth of hot mixture into eggs. Add to remaining hot mixture, stirring constantly. Spoon into prepared pie plate. Sprinkle with reserved crumb mixture and paprika. Bake at 400 degrees for 20 minutes, or until filling sets. Cut into wedges. Serve with fresh tomato salsa. Makes 6 servings.

American-Fried Potatoes

(NATE NEWTON)

6 medium potatoes
1/2 cup thinly-sliced onions
1/4 cup shortening
1 teaspoon salt
1/8 teaspoon pepper

Slice the potatoes; add onions. Heat shortening in a 9" frying pan. Add potato mixture; fry over medium heat, until golden brown, <u>turning frequently</u>. Season with salt and pepper. Makes 4 servings.

Sweet-Sour Cabbage

(ERIC BJORNSON)

5 cups shredded cabbage
4 slices bacon, diced
2 tablespoons brown sugar
1 small onion, diced

2 tablespoons flour
1/2 cup water
1/3 cup vinegar
salt and pepper

Cook cabbage in boiling, salted water for exactly 7 minutes *(will be tender-crisp)*; drain. In a skillet, sauté bacon; add brown sugar, onion, and flour, stirring *until completely blended with the fat*. Add water and vinegar; cook, stirring, until smooth and thick. Add seasonings, to taste; turn sauce over the drained cabbage. Toss over low heat until heated through. Serves 4 to 6, depending upon appetites.

Rosin-Baked Potatoes

(ERIK WILLIAMS)

Select the proper number of potatoes; if ordered from a large grocery, they may be ordered at a uniform 8-ounce size. This is the best serving size.

You will be able to buy powdered rosin from a chemical or pharmaceutical supply house; one pound will be ample for 25 potatoes.

Cut heavy-weight, aluminum foil into squares large enough to go around the potatoes. Make a double fold on top, and fold over 1/2" on each end.

Scrub the potatoes thoroughly. All of this preparation can be done hours ahead of time.

While the potatoes are still wet, roll them in the powdered rosin so that they are completely coated.

Wrap in the aluminum foil, making a double fold on top and on each end.

An 8-ounce potato, prepared in this fashion, will cook in exactly one hour at 375 degrees, and may be held in a very low oven (<u>under 325 degrees</u>) for another hour.

* They are truly delicious!

Kathy's Chicken Spaghetti

(KATHY WILSON)

1 chicken, or 5 or 6 chicken breasts
6 ounces ready-cut spaghetti
4 tablespoons margarine
1 onion, chopped
1 bell pepper, chopped
1 large jar diced pimiento, with juice
1 can cream of mushroom soup
1-1/2 cups sharp Cheddar cheese, grated
1 cup chicken broth

Stew chicken in salted water until tender; drain, reserving broth. Set aside 1 cup broth.

Cook spaghetti for 5 minutes in remaining broth; drain. Debone chicken; cut into bite-size pieces.

Sauté bell pepper and onion in margarine until tender. Mix all ingredients, except 1/2 cup cheese (reserved for topping).

Bake in covered casserole at 350 degrees for 30 minutes, or until heated through. Remove cover; sprinkle cheese on top of casserole. Continue baking until cheese melts.

Ravioli with Red Pepper Sauce

(JOHN JETT)

1 onion, chopped
1 clove garlic, crushed
1 tablespoon olive oil
1-1/2 pounds red bell peppers, chopped
1/2 cup vegetable stock
salt
freshly-ground black pepper
1 pound fresh, meat-filled ravioli
Parmesan cheese, freshly ground

In large pan, cook garlic and onion in oil until soft, but <u>not browned.</u> Add bell peppers, stock, salt, and pepper. Bring to boil. Cover the pan, reduce heat, and simmer for about 15 minutes, until bell peppers are soft.

Put the pepper mixture into a blender, or food processor; blend *until smooth.* Strain (sieve) the pepper mixture to remove any pieces of pepper skin.

Cook ravioli in boiling salted water for about 8 minutes, or according to packet instructions. Reheat the pepper sauce, if necessary. Divide among four warmed plates.

Drain ravioli; then, arrange on top of the pepper sauce. Serve sprinkled with Parmesan cheese.

Fettuccine Alfredo

(EULANDA BARNES)

fettuccine noodles
olive oil
1 carton whipping cream, and milk
Parmesan cheese (grated)
garlic clove
butter
shrimp/crab/chicken

Boil noodles with 1/2 teaspoon of olive oil; drain. In a separate pan, cook choice of meat with butter, garlic, salt, and pepper. Prepare alfredo sauce by combining 1 carton of whipping cream and butter; stir slowly. Begin adding cheese and small amounts of milk (to thin). Pour all ingredients in a large pan; simmer on low for 5 to 10 minutes. Enjoy!

Chris' Homemade Spaghetti

(CHRIS BONIOL)

1 package of chicken breasts
2 cans tomato paste
2 cans tomato sauce
2 cans tomatoes (whole)
1 tablespoon cooking oil
4 ribs celery
1 clove garlic
1 green bell pepper
1 onion
1/4 cup sugar
1/3 cup Worcestershire
 sauce

(CONTINUED)

Chris' Homemade Spaghetti -- (continued)

Dice celery, onion, garlic, and bell pepper. Heat 1 tablespoon cooking oil; then, add tomato paste. Add tomatoes and tomato sauce. Place diced vegetables in tomato sauce mixture.

Add chicken, sugar, and Worcestershire sauce. Chicken will cook as the sauce cooks.

Pasta with Fresh Tomatoes

(JIM MAURER)

4 cups diced, seeded tomatoes
3 tablespoons chopped, fresh oregano
3 tablespoons minced green onion
3 tablespoons fresh lemon juice
1 tablespoon olive oil
1 teaspoon coriander seeds, crushed
1/4 teaspoon salt
1/8 teaspoon crushed red pepper
2 garlic cloves, minced
6 cups hot, cooked vermicelli

In a large bowl, combine first 9 ingredients; mix well. Add pasta; toss well. Serve at room temperature.

Chicken Lasagna

(CRAIG BOLLER)

12 packaged lasagna noodles
1/2 cup egg substitute, or 2 eggs
1 container fat-free Ricotta cheese (15 ounces)
1/4 cup grated Parmesan cheese
1/4 teaspoon black pepper
2 cups chopped, fresh spinach
1 cup chopped zucchini, or yellow summer squash
1/2 cup chopped onion, or leek
1/2 cup finely-chopped carrot
1/2 cup chopped celery
1/2 cup chopped sweet red, yellow, or green pepper
1/4 cup snipped, fresh basil
3 large cloves garlic, minced
1 cup chicken broth
1/3 cup all-purpose flour
2 cups skim milk
1-1/2 cups chopped, cooked chicken
2 cups shredded, part-skim Mozzarella cheese

Cook pasta in boiling salted water for 8 to 9 minutes, or until almost tender. Drain; rinse with cold water. Drain again; set aside.

Stir together egg substitute or eggs, Ricotta and Parmesan cheeses, and black pepper. Stir in spinach; set aside.

For sauce: In a saucepan, cook zucchini, onion, carrot, celery, pepper, basil, and garlic in broth (about 10 minutes), or until carrot is tender. Do not drain. Whisk flour into milk; stir into vegetable mixture.

(CONTINUED)

Chicken Lasagna -- (continued)

Cook; stir until thickened and bubbly. Remove from heat; add chicken.

Layer 4 noodles, one-third of the Ricotta mixture, one-third of the sauce, and one-third of the Mozzarella in a greased 3-quart rectangular baking dish; repeat twice.

Bake, covered, at 350 degrees for 50 to 55 minutes, or until heated through. Let stand for 10 minutes before serving. Makes 10 to 12 servings.

Spinach Spaghetti Pie

(JOE AVEZZANO)

Crust Mixture:

6 ounces spaghetti
2 tablespoons butter, or margarine
2 eggs, beaten
1/3 cup grated Parmesan cheese

Cook spaghetti, according to package directions; drain. Stir in butter, eggs, and grated Parmesan cheese. Form spaghetti mixture into crust in pie plate.

(CONTINUED)

Spinach Spaghetti Pie -- (continued)

FILLING:

1 pound bulk Italian pork sausage
1/2 cup chopped onion
1 can tomato sauce (8 ounces)
1 cup small-curd cottage cheese
1 package cream cheese, softened (3 ounces)
2 eggs, beaten
1/4 cup grated Parmesan cheese
1 package frozen spinach, thawed and drained (10 ounces)
1/4 cup soft bread cubes
1 tablespoon butter, or margarine, melted

Cook sausage and onion; <u>drain off fat</u>. Stir in tomato sauce.

Spread sausage, onion, tomato mixture over crust.

Combine cottage cheese and cream cheese; stir in eggs and one-half of remaining Parmesan cheese mixture. Spoon on top of meat/tomato mixture.

Bake at 350 degrees for 20 minutes. Combine bread cubes, butter, and remaining Parmesan cheese; sprinkle on top. Bake another 8 to 10 minutes.

Fettuccine with Herbed Cheese Sauce

(GLORIA ALEXANDER)

3 tablespoons butter, or margarine
1/3 cup sliced green onions, with tops
1 clove garlic, minced
1 tablespoon all-purpose flour
1/2 teaspoon salt
1/2 teaspoon dried basil leaves, crushed
1/2 teaspoon dried oregano leaves, crushed
1/4 teaspoon pepper
1-3/4 cups milk
1 cup fancy supreme, shredded Mozzarella cheese
1 cup Ricotta cheese
3 tablespoons chopped, fresh parsley
fettuccine, or spaghetti (10 ounces)

In medium saucepan, melt butter over medium heat. Add onions and garlic; cook and stir until tender (about 5 minutes).

Stir in flour, salt, basil, oregano, and pepper. Gradually stir in milk. Heat until thick and bubbly, stirring occasionally. Remove from heat.

Add cheeses; stir until melted. Stir in parsley; keep warm.

Meanwhile, cook fettucine, according to package directions. Add cheese sauce; toss lightly to coat. Makes 6 servings.

Fried Rice

(SHANTE CARVER)

1 tablespoon oil
1/4 cup diced ham, or shrimp
1-1/2 cups cooked rice
1/4 cup diced, cooked vegetables
   (peas, carrots, green beans, etc.)
1 tablespoon thinly-sliced green onions
1 teaspoon soy sauce
1/2 teaspoon sesame oil
1/4 teaspoon salt
1 egg, beaten

Heat oil in skillet; sauté ham or shrimp for 30 seconds *on high heat.* Add rice; *lower heat to medium.* Cook for 2 minutes, stirring constantly. Stir in vegetables, soy sauce, sesame oil, salt, and egg; cook for 2 more minutes. Sprinkle with green onions. Makes 2 servings.

Stephen's Favorite Lasagna

(STEPHEN JONES)

1-1/2 pound ground chuck
1 pound ground sweet Italian sausage
1 tablespoon parsley
1 tablespoon basil
1/2 teaspoon salt
1 can tomatoes, chopped (16 ounces)
2 cans tomato paste (6-ounce can)
1 package lasagna noodles (10 ounces)

(CONTINUED)

Stephen's Favorite Lasagna -- (continued)

Brown meats; add all other ingredients. Cook, covered, for 45 minutes, stirring often.

Cook lasagna noodles, according to directions on package.

Cheese Mixture:

2 cartons large-curd cottage cheese
2 eggs, beaten
2 teaspoons salt
1/2 teaspoon pepper
1/2 cup Parmesan cheese, grated
2 tablespoons parsley flakes
1 pound Mozzarella cheese, sliced

Combine all ingredients of "Cheese Mixture", except Mozzarella cheese. Place one-half of the noodles in 13" x 9" x 2" pan; add one-half of cheese mixture, one-half pound Mozzarella cheese, and one-half the meat mixture. Repeat layers. Bake in 375-degree oven for 30 minutes, or until bubbly. Let stand for 10 to 15 minutes before serving. Makes 12 servings.

Baked Spinach Casserole

(TASHA TOLBERT)

2 packages frozen, chopped spinach
1 package onion soup mix
1 cup croutons
1 cup sour cream

Cook spinach, according to package directions; drain dry. Mix all ingredients together. Bake at 350 degrees for 20 to 30 minutes, or until bubbly. Serves 8.

Optional: top with Parmesan cheese.

Jim's "Cholesterol-Free" Potato Casserole

(JIM SCHWANTZ)

1-1/2 sticks of butter
1 can cream of chicken soup
1 cup chopped onion
1 teaspoon salt
1 teaspoon garlic salt
sour cream (16 ounces)
2 pounds hash browns, thawed
shredded Cheddar cheese (8 ounces)
1 cup corn flakes

(CONTINUED)

Jim's "Cholesterol-Free" Potato Casserole --
(continued)

Melt butter in chicken soup; remove from heat. Thoroughly mix in onions, salt, garlic salt, and sour cream; add to hash browns. Layer hash brown mixture with Cheddar cheese in casserole dish, saving some cheese for the top layer. Sprinkle corn flakes over the top *before baking.* Bake, <u>uncovered</u>, in a 13" x 9" casserole dish at 350 degrees for 90 minutes. Dot with butter, if desired.

Jayne Slade's Chili Beef Casserole

(JOYCE ZAMPESE)

1 pound ground beef
1 medium onion, chopped
1 clove garlic, minced
2 tablespoons chili powder
1 can chili-beef soup
1 cup sour cream
2 cups egg noodles, cooked
Parmesan and Cheddar cheese, grated

Brown meat, onion, garlic, and chili powder together. Stir in soup and sour cream; simmer for 5 minutes. Place one-half of noodles in a 1-1/2 quart casserole. *Sprinkle generously* with Parmesan cheese. Cover with one-half the meat. Repeat; top with Parmesan and Cheddar cheeses, covering all. Bake at 350 degrees for 30 to 45 minutes until bubbly and hot.

Potato Casserole

(MIKE McCORD)

2 pounds hash browns, thawed
1/2 cup butter, melted
1 can cream of chicken soup
small carton sour cream
2 tablespoons dried onion (or fresh, if desired)
1 teaspoon salt
2 teaspoons black pepper
2 cups grated Kraft American Deluxe cheese
2 cups crushed corn flakes
1/4 cup melted butter

Mix first 8 ingredients; put in buttered casserole dish. Set aside. Pour melted butter over crushed corn flakes; mix well. Top casserole with corn flake mixture. Bake at 350 degrees for 45 minutes to 1 hour.

Chicken/Stove-Top Casserole

(MANEESHA JONES)

4 boneless chicken breasts
1/2 cup melted butter
1 package stuffing mix
1 can cream of chicken soup
1 can cream of celery soup
2 soup cans of broth
1 cup bread crumbs

(CONTINUED)

Chicken/Stove-Top Casserole -- (continued)

Boil chicken breasts until tender; reserve broth. Chop chicken; combine with butter and stuffing in mixing bowl. In separate bowl, mix soups and 2 cans of reserved broth. Pour chicken mixture in 9" x 9" pan; next, pour soup over chicken. Top with bread crumbs. Bake for 45 minutes at 350 degrees. Serves 4 to 5 people. Easy and quick!

Delicious!

Russell's Deviled Crab Casserole

(RUSSELL MARYLAND)

1 cup milk
1 cup soft bread crumbs
2 cups cooked, flaked crab meat
2 hard-boiled eggs, mashed
1-1/2 teaspoons salt
1/3 teaspoon dry mustard
1/2 teaspoon lemon juice
1/8 teaspoon cayenne pepper
1/4 cup melted margarine
buttered bread crumbs

Combine milk and bread crumbs in a bowl; stir in crab meat and eggs. Blend in remaining ingredients, except crumbs. Place in a greased 10" x 6" x 2" baking dish; cover with buttered crumbs. Bake in 400-degree oven for 15 minutes. Makes 6 servings.

Biscuit-Topped Italian Casserole

(ROBERT JONES)

1 pound ground turkey (or lean ground beef)
1 frozen bag Birds Eye vegetables (corn, carrots, etc.)
1 large jar of favorite spaghetti sauce (or can be homemade)
1/2 cup sugar
3 or 4 cloves garlic, minced
1 cup Mozzarella cheese
1 can of refrigerated biscuits (10 biscuits)
1 cup Mozzarella cheese (or more)

Brown turkey; then, drain. Steam veggies, according to package directions.

In large saucepan, mix sauce, sugar, garlic, and cheese; simmer for 30 minutes. Add steamed veggies and turkey. Pour in large casserole dish. Top with <u>unbaked</u> biscuits; then, top with cheese. Serves 4 to 6 people.

Quick Chicken and Rice

(ALUNDIS BRICE)

1/2 cup wild rice, uncooked
1/2 cup white rice, uncooked
1 can cream of mushroom soup
1 can cream of celery soup
1-1/2 cups milk
6 halved chicken breasts
1/2 package dry onion soup mix

(CONTINUED)

Quick Chicken and Rice -- (continued)

Sprinkle rice on bottom of a lightly-greased baking dish. In saucepan, combine soups and milk; heat. Pour over rice. Top with chicken; sprinkle with onion soup mix. Cover; bake at 325 degrees for 2 hours.

Tasty Eggplant Casserole

(CLAYTON HOLMES)

1 medium eggplant
2 slices bacon, diced
1 medium onion, chopped
1 medium potato, grated
1 can creamy chicken mushroom soup, undiluted
  (10-3/4 ounces)
1/2 cup round, buttery cracker crumbs

Peel eggplant, and cut into 1" cubes. Cook in a small amount of boiling water for 10 minutes, or until tender. Drain well.

In a large skillet, fry bacon until crisp. Stir in onion and potato; cook until onion is tender. Add eggplant and soup, stirring well. Spoon into a lightly-greased 1-1/2 quart baking dish. Sprinkle with cracker crumbs. Bake at 350 degrees for 30 minutes. Makes 6 servings.

Ma Duke's Banana Split Pie

(TONY TOLBERT)

1 box Vanilla Wafers
2 packages cream cheese, softened (8 ounces)
2 cups powdered sugar
2 eggs
5 bananas
1-1/2 sticks butter, melted
Cool Whip (10 ounces)
1 can crushed pineapple, drained (15-1/4 to 16 ounces)
2/3 cup maraschino cherries
1 cup pecans

Mix together box of Vanilla Wafers (finely-crumbled) and stick of melted butter; spread on bottom of 13" x 9" cake pan, or a square bread pan.

Mix cream cheese, powdered sugar, and eggs; beat until smooth. Spread over wafers.

Slice bananas; put on top of first two layers. Spread drained pineapples over bananas.

Put Cool Whip over pineapples. Spread pecans and cherries over Cool Whip. Refrigerate for 8 hours, or overnight.

ENJOY!

Rice Pudding

(BROCK MARION)

1 cup white rice
2 cups water
2 tablespoons butter
1/4 teaspoon salt
2 tablespoons cornstarch
2 cups milk (may use 1 can evaporated milk, and enough regular milk, to yield 2 cups of liquid)
1 egg
1 cup sugar
1 teaspoon vanilla
lemon zest

In a large saucepan, boil water, butter, and salt; add dry rice. Boil 1 minute; reduce heat. Cover; simmer for 15 to 20 minutes, or until rice is done.

Meanwhile . . . put cornstarch in large mixing bowl; add just enough milk to dissolve cornstarch. Beat egg into cornstarch. Add remainder of milk and the sugar; mix well.

Pour milk mixture into cooked rice; return to low heat until thickened. Stir occasionally. Remove from heat. Stir in vanilla and zest of one lemon.

Pour onto serving platter; sprinkle with cinnamon.

Enjoy hot off the stove, or chilled.

Millionaire's Shortbread

(ROS DALRYMPLE)

1 pound butter
4 ounces castor sugar
6 ounces flour
1 can condensed milk
chocolate (8 ounces, or more)
2 tablespoons butter

In cuisinart, cream together butter, sugar, and flour; spread flat, about 1/2" thick, on cookie tray. Bake at 350 degrees for 30 minutes. <u>Do not brown.</u> Boil can of condensed milk in a saucepan of water for 2 hours. Top up with water -- *otherwise can will explode!* Condensed milk becomes caramel. Cool caramel; spread over cool shortbread. Melt chocolate and butter in microwave; spread over caramel. Cool; cut squares.

Quick and Easy Bread Pudding

(ROBERT FORD)

6 slices bread
1 cup sugar
3 eggs, beaten
1 teaspoon vanilla
1 teaspoon nutmeg
1 teaspoon cinnamon
3 cups milk
3/4 stick of butter, or margarine, melted

(CONTINUED)

Quick and Easy Bread Pudding -- (continued)

Preheat oven to 400 degrees. Soak bread in milk for 5 minutes. Add remaining ingredients to bread and milk mixture; mix by hand. Bake in 8" x 8" square cake pan for 1 hour.

* *To vary flavor, instead of vanilla, use almond or rum extract. Raisins are optional.*

Peach Pan Dowdy

(CRAIG BOLLER)

4 cups peaches, sliced (or other fruit)
1/4 cup sugar
1 teaspoon cinnamon

3 tablespoons shortening
3/4 cup sugar
1 teaspoon vanilla
2 tablespoons milk
1 cup flour
1 tablespoon baking powder

Put peaches in pan; sprinkle with sugar and cinnamon. Bake for 20 minutes at 400 degrees. Cream 3/4 cup sugar, shortening, vanilla, and milk until creamy. Add flour and baking powder to creamy mixture; spread on top of peaches. Bake, uncovered, for 25 minutes in 400-degree oven until brown.

Mini Blinis

(TROY AIKMAN)

2 packages cream cheese, softened (8-ounce package)
1/2 cup sugar
2 egg yolks
2 loaves thin-sliced white bread, crusts trimmed
   (1-pound loaves)
1 cup butter, melted
cinnamon and sugar, mixed to taste
sour cream
 jelly

Combine cream cheese, sugar, and yolks; beat until smooth.

Flatten each slice of bread with a rolling pin; spread with some of the cream cheese mixture. Roll jelly-roll fashion; dip in melted butter. Sprinkle with cinnamon-sugar mixture.

(If preparing ahead, place in single layer on baking sheet and freeze. When solid, transfer to plastic bags; return to freezer.)

When ready to serve, preheat oven to 400 degrees. Leave blinis whole, or cut each in half; place on baking sheet. Bake fresh blinis for 8 to 10 minutes, or frozen blinis *(thawing is not necessary)* for 10 to 15 minutes, or until light brown.

* *Serve hot, as snack or dessert, with sour cream and jelly on the side.*

Easy Chocolate Mousse

(NEILL ARMSTRONG)

1/3 cup strong, very hot coffee
1 package semi-sweet chocolate bits (6 ounces)
4 egg yolks
2 tablespoons "Creme de Cocoa" liqueur
4 egg whites
whipping cream

Combine hot coffee and chocolate in blender container. Cover; mix at high speed until very smooth. Add egg yolks and liqueur; beat again until very smooth. In large bowl, beat egg whites until stiff. Pour chocolate mixture over egg whites; fold in well. Pour into bowl, or in individual dishes; chill. Garnish with whipped cream. Makes 6 servings. MEN LOVE THIS!

Apple Cinnamon Crunch

(DENISE BATES)

1 can sliced apples, in juice (#10 can)
1 cup sugar
1 tablespoon lemon peel, finely shredded
1-1/4 cups flour
1 cup butter
1 teaspoon ginger
2 teaspoons cinnamon
1/2 teaspoon mace
2 cups rolled oats
2 cups brown sugar
2 teaspoons salt

(CONTINUED)

Apple Cinnamon Crunch -- (continued)

Stir together sugar, ginger, mace, 1/4 cup flour, and lemon peel. Toss apples with the sugar mixture; place in 2" hotel pan.

In another mixing bowl, combine oats, brown sugar, 1 cup of flour, 1 teaspoon cinnamon, and salt. Cut the butter into the oat mixture until the mixture is crumbly and the size of peas. Sprinkle the mixture over the apples.

Bake at 350 degrees for 40 minutes. When cool, cut the pan into 12 servings.

To serve: Microwave each serving for one minute, and top with one scoop of maple ice cream.

* *Served at Bill Bates' new restaurant,* "BILL BATES COWBOY GRILL".

Old-Fashioned Jelly Roll

(HURVIN MCCORMACK)

6 eggs, separated
2 cups sugar
5 tablespoons water
2 cups flour
1/4 teaspoon salt
2 teaspoons baking powder
jelly
powdered sugar

(CONTINUED)

Old-Fashioned Jelly Roll -- (continued)

Preheat oven to 350 degrees. Beat egg yolks and sugar in a bowl until thick; add water and mix well. Add flour, salt, and baking powder; mix until smooth. Fold in stiffly-beaten egg whites. Pour into 3 greased, shallow baking pans (12" x 8").

Bake until top springs back when lightly touched. Turn upside down onto damp towel <u>immediately</u>; spread with jelly. Roll from narrow end (as for jelly roll).

Cool on rack. Dust with powdered sugar. Slice and serve.

Coconut Flan

(CHARLIE WILLIAMS)

Caramel Topping:

1/2 cup granulated sugar
2 tablespoons water

For caramel topping, heat sugar and water in a small skillet, stirring constantly, until sugar melts and turns golden brown.

Pour syrup into a 1-quart baking dish, or into 6 custard cups, tipping to coat bottom and part way up sides.

Set dish aside while preparing custard.

(CONTINUED)

Coconut Flan -- (continued)

Custard:

2 cups milk
4 eggs
1/4 cup sugar
1/8 teaspoon salt
1/2 teaspoon vanilla
1/3 cup shredded, or flaked, coconut

For custard, scald milk. Beat eggs. Beat in sugar, salt, and vanilla. <u>Gradually</u> beat scalded milk into egg mixture. Strain into prepared baking dish, or custard cups. Sprinkle top with coconut. Place baking dish in pan containing hot water that comes at least 1" up sides of dish. Bake at 325 degrees for approximately 45 minutes in individual custard cups, or 1 hour in a baking dish.

Mrs. Blake's Marvelous Mango Fruit Parfait

(FREDA BLAKE)

This parfait has layers of bright red strawberries, vibrant orange mango, green kiwi, and deep red raspberries.

2 cups cubed mango (2 mangoes)
1/4 cup freshly-squeezed orange juice
24 strawberries, hulled (or more, if desired)
1 cup peeled and sliced kiwi (4 kiwis)
12 red raspberries

(CONTINUED)

Mrs. Blake's Marvelous Mango Fruit Parfait --
(continued)

Put the mangoes and orange juice in a blender; puree *(pulp, thick liquid)* until smooth.

Slice 20 of the strawberries, leaving 4 whole. Line the bottom of 4 balloon wine glasses with the sliced strawberries. Pour a thin layer of the mango puree over each, to cover.

Leaving 4 kiwi slices, layer the rest on top of the puree *(pulp, thick liquid)*. Divide the remainder of the mango puree among the glassed. Top each with a slice of kiwi, surrounded by raspberries.

Make a slit in each of the whole strawberries; position one on the rim of each glass. Cover with plastic wrap; refrigerate for 15 minutes.

A small amount of whipped cream may be added, if you desire. YUM!

Macadamia Nut Pie

(PONO TUINEI)

9" deep-dish pie shell, unbaked
3 eggs
1 cup sugar
1/2 tablespoon flour
1/3 cup melted butter
1 cup dark corn syrup
1-1/3 cups macadamia nut bits
1 teaspoon vanilla

Preheat oven to 400 degrees. Combine eggs, sugar, flour, butter, corn syrup, nuts, and vanilla. Pour into unbaked pie shell; bake for 15 minutes. Reduce temperature to 350 degrees; bake until golden brown, or an additional 40 to 45 minutes.

Chocolate Chess Pie

(ROSE MARYLAND)

1 cup sugar
2 eggs
1 stick margarine
1 square unsweetened chocolate (1 ounce)
1 teaspoon vanilla
8" pie shell, unbaked

Beat sugar and eggs until fluffy. Melt margarine and chocolate square over low heat; cool. Stir in sugar and egg mixture; mix well. Add vanilla. Put into unbaked pie shell; bake at 325 degrees for 35 minutes.

Original Applesauce Pie

(ERIC BJORNSON)

2 cans applesauce (16-1/2 ounce can)
1/2 cup sugar
1-1/2 teaspoons cinnamon
1/2 teaspoon nutmeg
3 tablespoons fresh lemon juice
6 tablespoons melted butter
2 frozen pie shells (8" or 9"), thawed

Cook the bottom pie crust at 400 degrees for 5 minutes. Blend together the first 6 ingredients; pour into the baked pie crust. Cover the applesauce mixture with the other pie crust, pressing loosely on the sides of the pie pan. Bake in pre-heated 350 degree oven for 30 minutes, or until brown. * *Delicious served hot and topped with ice cream.*

Strawberry Ice Box Pie

(LARRY BROWN)

1 package marshmallows (17 ounces)
1 box frozen strawberries, or 2 cups fresh strawberries
   (sweetened, to taste)
1 cup whipping cream
10" pie shell, baked

In double boiler, melt marshmallows with 2 tablespoons strawberry juice. Add strawberries; blend well. Chill for 2 hours. Whip cream; fold into mixture. Pour into baked pie shell; chill until firm.

Cream Puffs

(BROOKE HELLESTRAE)

Preheat oven to 450 degrees

1/2 cup butter
1 cup flour
4 eggs
1 cup boiling water
1/4 teaspoon salt

Melt butter in boiling water. Mix flour and salt together. Add flour mixture to boiling water, and water all at once; stir <u>quickly</u>. Keeping pan on the heat, stir mixture <u>constantly</u> until it forms a ball -- <u>be patient</u>! Remove mixture from heat.

Keeping mixture in pan, add eggs *(one at a time)*, beating into the mixture <u>vigorously</u> until smooth and all eggs are added.

Drop dough by *heaping tablespoons*, 3 inches apart, onto greased cookie sheet.

Bake at 450 degrees for 15 minutes -- turn oven down to 325 degrees for 25 minutes longer.

Remove from oven; cut in half. Open and leave side by side.

Turn oven off; put cream puffs in for 20 minutes to dry out. Cool on wire rack.

(CONTINUED)

Cream Puffs -- (continued)

Filling:

Mix vanilla instant pudding, according to box directions, but use one-half the amount of milk -- replaced with sour cream.

Frosting: 6 tablespoons milk
4 tablespoons cocoa
1/2 cup butter

Boil this mixture, stirring together. Add box (or so) powdered sugar; mix until smooth. Put filling inside shells. Drizzle with chocolate frosting on top. Sprinkle with crushed nuts.

Chocolate Fudge Pie

(MICHAEL IRVIN)

1 square of chocolate, or 1/4 cup cocoa
1 stick margarine, or butter
1 cup sugar
2 well-beaten eggs
5 tablespoons flour
1 teaspoon vanilla
1/2 cup pecans

In a saucepan, melt chocolate, or cocoa, and margarine. Add sugar; mix well. Add eggs, flour, vanilla, and pecans. Bake at 350 degrees for 25 minutes in buttered 8 or 9-inch pie plate. Serve warm (or cold) with whipped cream or ice cream.

Raisin Cream Pie

(ERIK WILLIAMS)

3/4 cup brown sugar
2 egg yolks, beaten
1 tablespoon melted butter
1 teaspoon vanilla
1-1/2 cups seeded raisins
1/3 cup cream
2 tablespoons vinegar
1/8 teaspoon salt
1/4 teaspoon cinnamon
1/4 teaspoon nutmeg
2 egg whites, beaten stiff

Prepare either a pastry, or a crumb-crust, shell in an 8" pie pan.

Combine sugar, egg yolks, and melted butter. Add raisins, cream, vinegar, salt, and spices.

Fold in stiffly--beaten egg whites; add vanilla.

Turn into the pie pan. If using a pastry crust, bake for 10 minutes at 425 degrees; then, bake 20 minutes longer at 350 degrees.

If using a crumb crust, bake for 30 minutes at 350 degrees.

Cool before serving.

Black Bottom Pie

(SHERMAN WILLIAMS)

1 tablespoon unflavored gelatin
1/4 cup cold water
2 cups rich milk
1/2 cup sugar
1-1/4 tablespoons cornstarch
4 eggs, separated
1-1/2 squares bitter chocolate, melted
1 teaspoon vanilla
1/4 teaspoon cream of tartar
1/2 cup sugar
1 tablespoon rum flavoring
whipped cream
9" pastry shell, or a rich crumb crust

Use a pastry shell, or a crust of either chocolate cookies or gingersnaps. Soak gelatin in cold water; scald the milk. Mix sugar and cornstarch together; add egg yolks, beating well. Stir this mixture into scalded milk; cook over low heat, or hot water, until the custard coats the spoon. <u>Stir constantly</u>. Take out one cup custard; add the melted chocolate to the cup of custard. Beat with rotary beater until cool; then, add vanilla. Pour into pie shell; chill. For the top layer, while remaining custard is still hot, blend in dissolved gelatin. Stir until completely blended. Beat egg whites until stiff; beat cream of tartar, half cup of sugar, and rum flavoring. Fold this meringue carefully into the soft custard. As soon as the chocolate layer is set, cover with the fluffy custard; chill.

* *Serve with a garnish of whipped cream.*

World's Best Cookies

(MIKE WOICIK)

1 cup butter
1 cup granulated sugar
1 cup brown sugar, packed
1 egg
1 cup vegetable oil
1 cup oatmeal, uncooked
1 cup crushed corn flakes
1/2 cup chopped pecans
1/2 cup shredded coconut
1 teaspoon vanilla
3-1/2 cups all-purpose flour
1 teaspoon baking soda
1 teaspoon salt

Cream butter and sugars until light and fluffy. Add egg; mix well. Add oil; mix well.

Add oatmeal, corn flakes, pecans, coconut, and vanilla; stir well. Add flour, baking soda, and salt; mix well.

Form into 1" balls. Place on ungreased baking sheet. Flatten with fork, dipped in water.

Bake at 350 degrees for 10 minutes. Cool on baking sheet for 10 minutes *before removing*. Makes about 9-1/2 dozen.

Caramel Brownies

(JAN McCORD)

50 light-colored caramels (14-ounce package)
1/3 cup evaporated milk
3/4 cup melted margarine
1 package German Chocolate Cake Mix
1/3 cup evaporated milk
1 cup chopped pecans
1 package semi-sweet chocolate chips (6 ounces)

Melt caramels and 1/3 cup milk in microwave; stir occasionally until melted. Set aside. Grease and flour 13" x 9" pan. Mix dry cake mix, butter, milk, and nuts *by hand* (until dough holds together). Press one-half of dough into prepared pan; reserve the rest of dough for the topping. Bake at 350 degrees for 6 minutes. Sprinkle chocolate chips over the baked crust; then, spread caramel mixture over the chocolate chips. Crumble rest of dough over the caramel mixture. Return to oven; bake for 15 to 18 minutes more. Cool for 30 minutes; cut into 36 bars. *Very rich!*

Date Kisses

(CHERYL BROWN)

3 egg whites
1 cup sugar
1 package dates
1/2 pound of pecans
1 teaspoon vanilla

(CONTINUED)

Date Kisses -- (continued)

Beat eggs until stiff; add sugar. Cook in double boiler until egg whites will stand in points when dropped from spoon. Remove from heat; add nuts, dates, and vanilla. Drop on well-greased cookie sheet about 2" apart. Bake for 45 minutes in a slow oven (300 degrees). Makes 36.

Jay's Cowboy Cookies

(JAY NOVACEK)

1 cup shortening
1 cup sugar
1 cup brown sugar
2 eggs
1 teaspoon vanilla
1-1/2 cups flour
1 teaspoon baking soda
1/2 teaspoon salt
1/2 teaspoon baking powder
2 cups oatmeal
1 cup chocolate chips

Cream shortening, sugar, and brown sugar together. Add eggs and vanilla to mixture. Then, add all the dry ingredients. Bake at 375 degrees for 8 to 10 minutes.

Coke Cake

(KATHY MAYS)

2 cups sugar
2 cups flour
1 teaspoon baking soda
2 sticks margarine
3 tablespoons cocoa
1 cup coke
2 eggs, beaten
1/2 cup buttermilk
1 teaspoon vanilla
1/2 cup miniature marshmallows

Mix sugar, flour, and baking soda together in a large bowl; set aside. Melt margarine, cocoa, and coke together; bring to a boil. Add coke mixture to sugar-flour mixture; mix well. Add beaten eggs, buttermilk, vanilla, and marshmallows to mixture; mix well. Pour into greased and floured 13" x 9" sheet pan. Bake about 40 to 45 minutes at 350 degrees. Ice while hot.

Icing: 1 stick butter
3 tablespoons cocoa
6 tablespoons coke
1 cup miniature marshmallows
1 teaspoon vanilla
1 box powdered sugar
1 cup chopped pecans

Stir butter, cocoa, coke, and marshmallows over low heat until marshmallows melt (<u>will stick easily</u>). Remove from heat; add vanilla, powdered sugar, and chopped pecans. *Stir until very smooth.*

Black Bottom Cupcakes

(DIANN AVEZZANO)

Betty Crocker Sour Cream Cake Mix -- Prepare cake mix, according to directions on the box.

Topping: 8 ounces cream cheese, softened
1 egg yolk, unbeaten
1/3 cup sugar
1/8 teaspoon salt
1 package chocolate chips (6 ounces)

Combine cream cheese, egg yolk, sugar and salt; mix well. Fold in chocolate chips; set aside. Fill cup cake tins/papers a little more than half-full; then, put about 1 teaspoon topping in each. Bake at 400 degrees for 15 to 20 minutes. * *Can also bake in Bundt pan -- at temperature and time listed on the cake mix box.*

Sand Tarts

(TINA HOWELL-WILLIAMS)

1 stick butter
1 tablespoon sugar
1-1/2 teaspoons vanilla
1 cup flour
1/2 cup chopped pecans
powdered sugar

Mix butter, sugar, and vanilla. Flour nuts; put two mixtures together. Roll in small bars (about the size of your thumb). Bake at 425 degrees for about 15 minutes. When done, roll in sugar *while very hot*. Makes 3 dozen.

German Sweet Chocolate Cake

(MARY SMITH -- MOTHER OF EMMITT SMITH)

1 package Baker's German Sweet Chocolate (4 ounces)
1/2 cup water
2 cups flour
1 teaspoon baking soda
1/4 teaspoon salt
1 cup margarine, or butter, softened
2 cups sugar
4 egg yolks
1 teaspoon vanilla
1 cup buttermilk
4 egg whites

Preheat oven to 350 degrees. Line bottoms of three 9" round cake pans with wax paper. Microwave chocolate and water in large bowl *(useable for microwave)* on high for 1-1/2 to 2 minutes, or until chocolate is almost melted; stir halfway through heating time. *Stir until chocolate is completed melted.**

Mix flour, baking soda, and salt together; set aside.

In large bowl, beat margarine and sugar with electric mixer *(on medium speed)* until light and fluffy. Add egg yolks, one at a time, beating well after each addition. Stir in chocolate mixture and vanilla.

Add flour mixture <u>alternately</u> with buttermilk, beating after each addition until smooth.

(CONTINUED)

German Sweet Chocolate Cake -- (continued)

In another large bowl, beat egg whites with electric mixer (on high speed) until stiff peaks form. Gently stir into batter.

Pour into prepared pans. Bake for 30 minutes, or until cake springs back when lightly touched in center. Immediately run spatula between cakes and sides of pans. Cool for 15 minutes; remove from pans. Remove wax paper; cool completely on wire racks.

Spread "Coconut-Pecan Frosting" between layers and over the top of cake. Makes 12 servings.

* Top of stove preparation: Heat chocolate and water in heavy 1-quart saucepan on very low heat, stirring constantly until chocolate is melted and mixture is smooth. Remove from heat; continue as above.

Coconut-Pecan Frosting:

1 cup evaporated milk
1 cup sugar
3 egg yolks, slightly-beaten
1/2 cup butter
1 teaspoon vanilla
1-1/3 cups coconut
1 cup chopped pecans

In saucepan, combine milk, sugar, egg yolks, butter, and vanilla. Cook over medium heat, stirring constantly, until mixture thickens (about 12 minutes); remove from heat. Add coconut and pecans. Beat until cool and of spreading consistency.

Alabama Fruit Cake

(SHERMAN WILLIAMS)

1/2 pound chopped, candied pineapple
1 pound chopped dates
1/2 pound candied cherries
1 quart pecans
1/2 teaspoon salt
1 cup flour
1 cup sugar
1 teaspoon baking powder
4 eggs
1/2 cup sherry
1 teaspoon vanilla

Dredge fruit and nuts in the dry ingredients.

Beat eggs until light and fluffy; pour over fruit/nut mixture. Mix mixture well with your hands.

Add sherry and vanilla. Mix with hands again.

Bake in very slow oven at 275 degrees for about 2 hours in a 9" tube pan. Cool.

Store in tight container. Dribble a little sherry over cake each day.

* If container is tin, wrap cake in foil to prevent rust on cake.

Prune Cake

(DOROTHY BOLING -- GRANDMOTHER OF
MICHAEL BATISTE)

1 cup soft butter
2 cups sugar
4 eggs
1 cup cooked prunes *
3 cups flour
1/4 teaspoon salt
1 teaspoon soda
1/2 teaspoon baking powder
1-1/2 teaspoons cinnamon
1 teaspoon nutmeg
1 teaspoon allspice
1 cup buttermilk
1 teaspoon vanilla
1 cup nuts (optional)

Cream butter and sugar together; add eggs. Beat until creamy. Add prunes; mix.

Add <u>alternately</u> the sifted dry ingredients and buttermilk, mixed with vanilla. Beat until all ingredients are smooth.

Pour into a greased tube pan. Bake at 350 degrees about 50 minutes, or until golden brown and springy to touch.

* *Use pitted prunes.*

Heavenly Bars

(YVETTE NOVACEK)

2 sticks margarine
4 tablespoons cocoa
2 cups sugar
1-1/2 cups flour
4 eggs
1 cup nuts
1 package miniature marshmallows
1/2 teaspoon vanilla

Cream margarine and sugar together; add eggs, *one at a time.* Add cocoa, flour, and chopped nuts; mix well. Pour into a 13" x 9" pan; bake for 30 minutes at 350 degrees. Cover with marshmallows. Let melt and cool.

Frosting: 4 tablespoons cocoa
1 stick margarine
3 cups powdered sugar
5 tablespoons evaporated milk

Mix cocoa, margarine, powdered sugar, and evaporated milk together; mix until creamy. Frost; cut into delicious bars.

Mint/Chocolate Chip/ Cream Cheese Brownies

(DARYL JOHNSTON)

3 cups Tollhouse mint -chocolate morsels (18 ounces)
4 tablespoons butter
1 cup all-purpose flour
1 teaspoon baking powder
1/2 teaspoon salt
4 eggs
3 teaspoons vanilla
2 cups sugar
1 cup of chocolate chips
Philadelphia Cream Cheese, softened (6 ounces)
2 eggs, beaten

Grease and lightly flour a 13" x 9" x 2" baking pan. Melt butter and chocolate; cool. Stir together flour, baking powder, and salt. In a mixing bowl, beat eggs and 2 teaspoons of vanilla; gradually add 1-1/2 cups of the sugar. Continue beating 4 eggs, until thick and lemon-colored. Add dry ingredients; beat until well combined. Stir in chocolate. Stir in 1 cup of mint chips.

In separate bowl, beat Philadelphia Cream Cheese and remaining one-half cup sugar until fluffy. Add remaining 2 eggs and 1 teaspoon vanilla; beat until smooth.

Spread one-half chocolate batter in pan. Then, pour cheese mixture over chocolate batter. Top with chocolate batter. Swirl layers, if desired. Bake at 350 degrees about 40 minutes. Cool; cut into bars.

Amaretto Bundt Cake

(SHARLENE EDDY)

1 box butter cake mix (18-ounce box)
1 box instant vanilla pudding mix (3.4-ounce box)
4 eggs
1/2 cup vegetable oil
1/2 cup water
1/2 cup Amaretto liqueur
1 cup chopped almonds

Preheat oven to 350 degrees. Combine all ingredients in large bowl of electric mixer; beat for 10 minutes.

Pour into greased and floured Bundt pan. Bake for 1 hour.

Glaze: 1/4 cup margarine, or butter
1/2 cup granulated sugar
2 tablespoons water
2 tablespoons Amaretto liqueur

In small saucepan, mix margarine or butter, sugar, and water; bring to a boil. Boil for 2 minutes. Add Amaretto.

When cake is done, pierce with a fork. Pour one-half of glaze over cake; let sit for 5 minutes. Invert and remove from pan. Pierce remaining top and sides of cake; pour remaining glaze over cake. Cover; allow to set for at least 8 hours, if possible.

Black Walnut Devil's Food Cake

(AMY BUCHANAN)

3 squares of sweet chocolate
2/3 cup boiling water
2-1/4 cups flour
3/4 teaspoons salt
1-1/2 teaspoons baking powder
3 whole eggs, beaten lightly
6 tablespoons butter
1-1/2 cups sugar
1/4 cup sour milk
1 teaspoon vanilla

Melt sweet chocolate squares over hot water; add boiling water. Stir well. Add 1-1/2 teaspoons baking soda; mix well. Cream butter and sugar; add eggs alternately with sour milk and flour. Add vanilla; then, add melted chocolate. Bake in three layers.

Black Walnut Filling:

1 cup brown sugar
6 to 8 egg yolks
pinch of salt
1/2 cup flour
1 cup thick cream
1/2 cup ground English walnuts
1/4 teaspoon walnut flavoring

(CONTINUED)

Black Walnut Devil's Food Cake -- (continued)

Cook until thick; cool. Then, put between layers of cake. If desired, put some on top of cake.

Fudge Frosting:

1 square unsweetened chocolate
2/3 cup cold milk
2 scant cups sugar
2 tablespoons white syrup
dash salt
2 tablespoons butter
1 teaspoon vanilla

Add chocolate to milk; place over low heat. Cook until mixture is smooth.

Add sugar, syrup, and salt; cook until it forms a ball in cold water.

Remove from heat; add butter. Beat until firm enough to spread over cake.

Marki's Fruit in a Cone

(MARKI ZIMMER)

1 large waffle cone
3 cut-up strawberries
1/4 cup fresh raspberries
1 teaspoon honey
1/2 cut-up banana
1/4 cup grapes, seedless
granola

Place fruits in bowl together *(you can choose favorite fruits, if desired)*; mix well.

Fill waffle cone. Drizzle honey over the top; sprinkle with granola.

* Hint: Make these extra fun by dipping cones in melted chocolate before preparing them.

Kid's Play Dough

(BROOKE HELLESTRAE)

1 cup flour
1/4 cup salt
2 tablespoons cream of tartar
1 cup water
2 teaspoons food coloring (any color)
1 tablespoon vegetable oil

(CONTINUED)

Kid's Play Dough -- (continued)

Mix flour, salt, and cream of tartar in medium pot. Add water, food coloring, and oil; stir over medium heat for 3 to 5 minutes. The mixture will look like a mess -- will eventually turn into "dough".

When the mixture forms a ball in center of pot, turn off heat; cool down.

Take out of pot; put on floured surface. Squish it and punch it around -- knead well -- *the kids will love it!*

When done, store in __airtight__ container in refrigerator.

RECIPE INDEX

RECIPE INDEX

RECIPES INDEX -- continued

RECIPES INDEX -- continued

RECIPES INDEX -- continued

RECIPES FROM ADMINISTRATION,
INDIVIDUAL PLAYERS,
and COACHES (and THEIR WIVES)